On the Prayer of Jesus

a gift from
Renaldo Romero
2006

THE IBIS WESTERN MYSTERY TRADITION SERIES

The heritage of all Western spirituality, both open and esoteric, and all the systems, theories, and practices that relate to it, are drawn from a single source: the Judeao-Christian spiritual tradition. This tradition has yet deeper roots in the distinctive religious faiths of the great civilzations of Egypt, Greece, and Mesopotamia.

At the heart of all these great traditions lies their ultimate goal: the spiritual regeneration of humanity. There is more than one Way to its attainment, and it is the totality of the many paths that lead us back to our primal source that constitutes the Western Mystery Tradition. They are encapsulated in the countless texts that enshrine and reflect the work of the inspired men and women who have dedicated their lives to preserving, interpreting, and transmitting this tradition.

Many of these text have become a part of the canon of Western literature, but there are many others that have been unjustly neglected, hidden in times of persecution, or have simply gone unrecognized. Some record exalted inner experiences, some are guides to esoteric practice, while others are speculative studies of esoteric knowledge and spiritual wisdom. All of them have one feature in common: an inherent power to enrich us spiritually.

It is from rare printed versions of these unknown or forgotten texts, and from studies of them, that the Ibis series of classics of the Western Mystery Tradition is drawn.

—The Editors of Ibis Press

Ignatius Brianchaninov

On the Prayer of Jesus

Translated by
Father Lazarus

Foreword by
Allan Armstrong

Introduction by
Alexander d'Agapeyeff

Ibis Press
An Imprint of Nicolas-Hays, Inc.
Berwick, Maine

Published in 2006 by
Ibis Press, an imprint of
Nicolas-Hays, Inc.
P. O. Box 1126
Berwick, ME 03901-1126
www.nicolashays.com

Distributed to the trade by
Red Wheel/Weiser, LLC
65 Parker St
Newburyport, MA 01950-4600
www.redwheelweiser.com

Library of Congress Cataloging-in-Publication Data available on request.

ISBN 0-89254-120-2

VG

Cover design by Kathryn Sky-Peck.

Printed in the United States of America

11	10	09	08	07	06
6	5	4	3	2	1

The paper used in this publication meets the minimum requirements of the American National Standard for Information Sciences—Permanence of Paper for Printed Library Materials Z39.48–1992 (R1997).

CONTENTS

FOREWORD

St. Ignatius Bryanchaninov, Bishop of the Caucasus and the Black Sea, and the author of this book, was born Dimitrii Bryanchaninov in February 1807 of an aristocratic Russian family in the Vologda province of Russia, a region well known for its arts and crafts, especially an exquisite lace, for which it is still famous. His father, a child of the Enlightenment with European tastes and ambition, was a member of Emperor Paul I's court and an active Freemason of Pozdeev's circle. In 1812, after the end of the war with Napoleon, he and his wife, Sofia Aleksandrovna, left St. Petersburg to settle on the family estate in the Vologda province. Dimitrii's upbringing was genteel and very strict. Indeed, it is said that "the Brianchaninovs were a typical aristocratic family in which relations between the children and the parents were formal and reserved. The memoirs of Bishop Ignatii's niece conveyed the atmosphere of domestic hierarchy, puritan discipline, and emotional distance."[1]

Because Dimitrii's health was never robust—it was to cause him problems throughout his life—he received a good education at home and in due course entered the Imperial School of Engineers in St. Petersburg, where he soon proved himself to be an exceptional pupil who was popular with both his professors and fellow pupils. The combination of his brilliance and aristocratic background probably facilitated his introduction to the house of Alexei Olenin, president of

---

[1] Dr. Irina Paert, "The Unmercenary Bishop" in *Slovinia* 9, no. 2, p. 101.

the Imperial Academy of Arts, and through him he came into contact with the elite of Russian society. Dimitrii also attracted the attention of the Grand Duke Nicholas, the future Emperor Nicholas I, who was to be so influential in shaping his career; indeed, at that point in time, Dimitrii seemed to have been set for a brilliant career in the secular world, except for the fact that from an early age he had been drawn to the religious life, particularly to monasticism. This aspiration was discouraged by his family, particularly by his father, who was deeply influenced by Masonic esoteric thought concerning universal Christianity,[2] and who probably expected his son to follow in his footsteps. However, while at the Imperial School of Engineers, Dimitrii began to visit the monks of the Valaam Priory in St. Petersburg, with whom he engaged in lengthy discussions, and where he took communion on a weekly basis, an act that was thought to be a little eccentric as the fashion of the time was to commune far less frequently. Indeed, his fellow students at the Imperial School communed no more that once a year.

Through the influence of the monks of the Valaam Priory, Dimitrii was introduced to Fr. Athanasius, a learned confessor of the Lavra[3] of St. Alexander Nevsky in St. Petersburg. Under the guidance of Athanasius, Dimitrii began studying theology, the writings of the Holy Fathers of the Church, and other mystical works. Inevitably, his father heard of his son's interest in monastic life, and did everything he could to change his son's mind, including bringing influence to bear upon the Primate of St. Petersburg, complaining that Father

---

[2] *Ibid.* ". . . the enlightened men of Brianchaninov's cohort believed that there was a difference between the initiated, who were awakened and called to introspection, on the one hand, and the 'lower class of recently catechised people', who were satisfied with ritual worship in churches, on the other hand." p. 101.

[3] A lavra is a community of monks.

Athanasius was unwisely encouraging Dimitrii to join the monastic orders. Consequently, Athanasius was forbidden to engage with the young Dimitrii. This might well have been the end of the matter but Dimitrii, who was obviously made of sterner stuff, refused to comply and personally confronted the primate, informing him that his convictions were not only serious but deeply rooted. His argument must have been convincing because he was allowed to continue his connection with the monks of the Lavra of St. Alexander Nevsky.

On passing his final examinations, Dimitrii Bryanchaninov was commissioned as an officer in the Engineers and in the winter of 1826 he was posted to the fortress of Dunaburg.[4] Shortly after his arrival there, he became seriously ill and was declared unfit for military service. He was then granted a discharge. Upon his discharge from the military, Dimitrii sought to fulfil his calling to live the life of a monk. From the beginning he was "cut off" by his family, and it is said he disguised himself as a peasant and sought entrance to the Svirsky monastery,[5] where he was received with kindness and put to work in the kitchen. Here he came under the spiritual guidance of the renowned Staretz Leonid Nagolkin.[6] Nagolkin moved to the Ploshchansky monastery in the province of Orel and about a year or two later Dimitrii followed him so that he could continue to study with him. However, Nagolkin moved again to the Optino monastery where he was to become its first great staretz. This monastery was pivotal in the spiritual revival taking place in Russia in the first half of the 19th century, and was frequently visited by distinguished thinkers, philosophers, and writers seeking spiritual guidance and instruction; among them were such

---

4   Now known as Daugavpils, Latvia.

5   Situated deep in the woods of the St. Petersburg countryside.

6   A "staretz" is the Russian equivalent of a spiritual elder.

luminaries as Gogol, Leo Tolstoi and Dostoievski. Dimitrii again followed him, but unfortunately the austere regime of the monastery undermined his health to the point where he could do nothing but withdraw.

Thus Dimitrii returned home, to the delight of his parents, who thought the young man had wearied of the monastic life. However, they were soon disillusioned, for before long he became a postulant in the Kirilov Novoesky monastery, where, after a short time, he again became ill and was forced to leave because of his health. It was a difficult time for him, and it is possible to see his early years in the monastic environment as a trial that tested his resolve to the limit. It is arguable that his constitution was not up to the austere requirements of the monastic life; nevertheless, his perseverance had been noted and he was eventually admitted into the Semigorodsky monastery by Stefan, the bishop of Vologda. In June 1831, Dimitrii renounced the world and Stefan received his profession as a monk, giving him the name of Ignatius after St. Ignatius Theophoros, the first-century bishop of Antioch. Within a year, he was ordained to the priesthood and sent to revive the monastery of Pelshem Lopotov. Although he accomplished a great deal at the monastery, the cold and damp conditions of the marshlands wherein the monastery was situated made him very ill, and once again his future looked bleak. He was then offered a more congenial position as abbot of the Ugreshky monastery, but whether he would have taken the position or not we shall never know for it was at this crucial moment that the Emperor Nicholas I, hearing of Ignatius's predicament, beckoned him to St. Petersburg where the emperor is reported to have said to him, "You are my debtor for the education which I arranged for you and for my love for you. You did not want to serve me where I intended to send you. You selected another road by your own free will. You will repay your debt to me in that very field. I appoint you to Sergiev Monastery, I want you to live there and make the monastery a model for the capital."[7] Thus, at the request of the emperor, Ignatius was raised by the Holy Synod to the dignity of archimandrite and appointed superior of the Sergiev monastery, some seventy miles northwest of St. Petersburg. Archimandrite Ignatius arrived at the monastery in January, 1834, where he served as abbot for almost twenty-five years. He found the monastery in a state of dereliction and with barely a dozen monks living within it, but with their aid and with the support of the Emperor, he was able to put the monastery back into good order. Slowly but surely, the number of monks increased and in time, Ignatius instituted splendid services supported by a first-class choir, organised lectures and conferences, and wrote many essays and short treatises for monks and lay folk alike.

Undoubtedly, as a religious, Ignatius spent considerable time in prayer, but his preference had ever been to live the life of a contemplative; indeed it is evident in his writings that his spirit longed for the stillness of the desert, where he might without interruption engage his entire being in the prayer of the heart. Thus his life in the Sergiev monastery, which was growing in reputation, did not truly suit him. He was too accessible to the many visitors that came from far and wide, from both the court and the intelligentsia of his day. He became the spiritual director of many people, including not only members of the monastic community but also many people in the secular world. This was to take its toll and inevitably, his health began to deteriorate. On several occasions he applied for a transfer to a more contemplative environment, but his requests, opposed by the emperor, were turned down by the Holy Synod, although he was eventually given leave to retire for the best part of a year to the

---

[7] *Žizeopisanija*, p. 321.

Nicolo-Babaev monastery in Kostroma in order to rest and recuperate.

When the Emperor Nicholas I died in 1856, Ignatius once more sought authorization to retire to the Optino monastery, to live the contemplative life. The response of the court and the Holy Synod was, however, to make him a bishop. Consequently, in the month of October 1857, Ignatius was consecrated as bishop of the Caucasus and the Black Sea, and in 1858 he took up residence in his new diocese, where he soon found that there was an immense amount of work to be done; not the least being to build an Episcopal residence. Once more, he set about establishing order in an undisciplined environment, something at which he evidently excelled. However, this time providence had decided that he had done enough, for within two years of his arrival in Stavropol he came down with smallpox and his health finally broke. Reluctantly the Holy Synod accepted the resignation of this able servant and appointed him Superior of the Nicolo-Babaev monastery, where he took residence in 1861.

In his retirement, Ignatius continued with his literary work, giving final shape to his ascetical and mystical doctrine. His writings were eventually published in four volumes in St. Petersburg between 1865 and 1867.[8] His work was written principally for his fellow monks, and contains a wealth of important material concerning the spiritual life of the monastic. The first volume describes how spiritual aspirants should follow Christ; how they should read the Gospels and study the teachings of the Fathers. He also gives instruction concerning the use of prayer, particularly the Jesus Prayer. The second volume contains ascetical essays in the form of instructions and meditations concerning the spiritual life, one of which is the basis of the present book. The third volume contains many

---

[8] Episkop Ignatij, *Socinenija,* 4 vols. (St. Petersburg, 1865–1867).

of his ascetical sermons. The fourth and last volume, titled an "Offering to Contemplative Monks," contains spiritual advice and rules for the behaviour of monks.

In the winter months of 1867, his health began to fail, and on Easter Sunday, 1867 he took leave of the community to prepare for his death. On April 30, 1867, in his sixty-first year, Bishop Ignatius Bryanchaninov died. He was canonised by the Russian Orthodox Church in 1988.

It is not possible in this brief introduction to explore the full extent of Ignatius Brianchaninov's influence upon the revival of Russian spirituality, but one should bear in mind that he was, together with the elders of the Optino monastery, a tremendous influence upon the evolution of modern orthodox culture. This was in part due to his privileged upbringing and secular education, which enabled him to play a significant role on many levels in the re-Christianisation of a Russian society struggling to reconcile the ever encroaching influences of the Western Enlightenment' with the traditional spiritual values of Eastern orthodoxy. He was the first great orthodox theologian to confront directly the problem of preserving the orthodox Christian tradition in a world that was striving to overthrow and dismiss it or else redefine it in a way that made it compatible with an increasingly secular way of life and thinking. Indeed, it may justly be said that Ignatius was not so much a hard-line purist seeking a return to a past "golden-age" as he was a reformer seeking to integrate the essence of Eastern orthodoxy into a radically changing world.

Well-grounded in the ascetic disciplines and writings of the Holy Fathers, Bishop Ignatius grasped the essence of the ancient monastic traditions of the orthodox Church. Through his love of solitude and prayer, as well as teaching by his own example, he was able to pass on to those in his charge a way of life that had been central to Eastern Christianity for almost two thousand years. The guiding principle about which his work turned was the unique spiritual discipline of contemplative prayer known as the Prayer of the Heart, or "The Jesus Prayer" and the teachings of the spiritual masters of the Church, whose writings are to be found in the classic spiritual work, the Philokalia.[9]

This Prayer of the Heart, *Jesus Christ, Son of God, Have mercy upon me, a sinner,* is the prayer that constitutes the core discipline of a mystical tradition that lies at the heart of the monastic life of the Eastern Church. This particular tradition, known by the name of Hesychasm, is generally accepted as having existed in one form or another within the Eastern Church from apostolic times. The word "Hesychasm" is derived from the Greek word *hesuchia* (ησυχια), "quietness," and has come to signify the life of a solitary monastic dedicated to the spiritual work of contemplative prayer. Hesychasm has had many forms in its evolution, but was given its most distinctive form in the 14th century by St. Gregory Palamas (1296–1359).[10] This contemplative way of life, which had been fostered from the earliest days of the Church, found in the turbulent years of the third century a relatively peaceful and fertile soil in the desert lands of the Levant (Egypt, Syria, and Palestine). The inhospitable nature of the desert provided the ideal environment for Christian ascetics seeking to live the spiritual life. Over the course of time, some of these ascetics formed the loose-knit com-

---

[9] The Philokalia is a collection of spiritual texts connected with the spiritual life of the hesychast and the practice of the Jesus Prayer, written between the fourth and fifteenth centuries, which were compiled by St. Nikodimos of the Holy Mountain and St. Makarios of Corinth and published in five volumes in the late eighteenth century. *Philokalia* means "love of beauty."

[10] A leading exponent of Hesychasm, St. Gregory Palamas supported the hesychast claim to experience God, interpreting the communication in terms of the uncreated light experienced by the disciples at the Transfiguration of Christ.

munities that were to evolve into institutional monasteries which—during the fourth century, inspired by such luminaries as St. Anthony, Macarius, Pachomius, and Basil the Great—flowered and spread rapidly throughout the Greco-Roman world, deeply influencing and shaping the spiritual life of both Eastern and Western Christianity.

The monasticism of these desert fathers was unquestionably strongly ascetic, and through their influence, asceticism became a fundamental part of Eastern Christian life, especially in the life of the hesychast, in which poverty, fasting, and prayer are so important. The word asceticism is derived from the Greek ασκησις (exercise, or training), and was originally used by the Stoic philosophers to denote a system of athletic practices aimed at combating vices and developing virtues. This form of asceticism was a discipline that used psycho-spiritual processes to separate the soul from the body and its negative influence. This discipline had long been established in the Greco-Roman world and was given a fresh impetus by the Neo-Platonists; but, in Christianity the ascetic process was aimed at achieving purification not by *separation* but through *unification*—the unification of the body, soul, and spirit in Christ. For the Hesychast, this ascesis was a means of training the whole person in a spiritual discipline, central to which was the practice of prayer according to the instruction of St. Paul, who in his first letter to the Thessalonians advocates that all who aspire to the spiritual life should "Pray without ceasing" (I Thess. 5:17). Thus, in the desert communities of the fourth century, many forms of "ceaseless prayer" were developed, invariably consisting of a short formula that was often no more than a single word or name, and never more than a phrase or two. The value of such a formula rests in the fact that such prayers may be used habitually, thereby becoming a natural and self-perpetuating reflex that sublimates the incessant mental noise that is our common experience of the mundane world, and prepares the mind for the communion with the divine substrate of our existence—God. One mode, still in use today, and the subject of this book, is the Jesus Prayer.

Thus, in the silence of the desert the core ascetic disciplines of Hesychasm were established, and in this environment the Prayer of the Heart—the alternative name for the Jesus Prayer—emerged, the practice of which, Ignatius informs us in the opening chapter of this book, rests upon the instruction of the Lord Jesus Christ Himself, who said "And whatsoever you shall ask in my name, this will I do, that the Father may be glorified in the Son. If you shall ask anything in my name, I will do it" (John 14:13–14). To the aspiring Christian following the path of contemplation these words comprise a divine institution that must be followed, and in the Eastern Church this has been the case from the earliest times. It has become the heart of Hesychasm.

The notion of ceaseless prayer may appear incomprehensible to many, particularly to those who look upon prayer as a form of plea-bargaining with God, but for the desert fathers and all who succeeded them, including Ignatius Bryanchaninov, prayer means something else entirely. It signifies the secret language of the soul, a language that synthesises thought, image, and emotion into one thing, in a manner that transcends the limitations of our mundane existence. This kind of prayer requires the complete attention of our consciousness, focussed upon the ultimate object and purpose of life: God. It is then, in effect, the most natural and practical expression of our love, by which we are able to be joined "in one spirit" with God.

This need to pray unceasingly is emphasised frequently by the early Church Fathers. For example, Origen, who in the early part of the third century wrote at some length about the need to pray constantly in his book *On Prayer*, says, "And he prays 'constantly' who unites prayer with the deeds required and right deeds with prayer. For the only way we can accept the command to "Pray constantly" as referring to a real possibility is by saying that the entire life of the saint taken as a whole is a single great prayer."[11] For the hesychast this is the main objective of the ascetic life and the Jesus Prayer is the ultimate tool whereby it may be achieved, but the life of the Hesychast has ever been an arduous one, suitable only for an inspired few. Even in Ignatius's time, few people could tolerate the physical and psychological hardship involved in such a life. Yet this has never stopped the many individuals, whose secular commitments forbade them to withdraw from the mundane world, from engaging with the discipline of the Jesus Prayer.

Ignatius Bryanchaninov understood this and although he wrote mainly for the monastic, he wrote many essays for laypeople, of which this little book is a remarkable example. It is quite short and easy to read, yet nevertheless demonstrates great power in the way it gently introduces the reader to its subject matter. Ignatius manages to synthesize both the requirement for practical instruction in the methods involved in Hesychasm, and the need for spiritual guidance in a way that enables anyone to engage with the sublime spirituality of the Jesus Prayer. The book is divided into seventeen chapters, in the first six of which Ignatius teaches us about the power of the name of Jesus and the right way of approach to using it. He informs us that the Jesus Prayer is as much about preparation as it is about use; and although it may seem mantra-like, it is not simply a mantra to be blindly chanted

---

[11] Rowan Greer, trans., *Origen: Classics of Western Spirituality* (Mahwah, NJ: Paulist Press, 1979), p. 104.

so many times before the effect might be felt as an endorphin rush. He quietly informs us that such prayer is holy and that "holy prayer" is based on a state of being that is produced by living one's life according to the commandments; and cannot exist in a soul that lives otherwise. Indeed, there are countless references pointing to the fact that even in the monastic environment of the early Church, it was generally forbidden for monks to engage prematurely in the Prayer of the Heart. However, it is true to say that the preparation of the soul for engaging in this prayer applies equally to both the layperson and the monastic. With this in mind, Ignatius introduces us to the teachings of St. John of the Ladder,[12] one of the spiritual fathers of the Eastern Church, as he believed that the method proposed by St. John was not only safe, but "suitable for all Christians living piously and seeking salvation." From chapter seven onwards, Ignatius introduces us to the central teachings of the spiritual masters of the Eastern Church, as defined in the *Philokalia*. Chapter by chapter he introduces us to some of the most evocative teachings ever written concerning the Christian way of spiritual evolution; teachings that are in the main unknown outside the Eastern Church.

The methodology of the Jesus Prayer has been explained over the course of time in various ways and in varying degrees of complexity, but the essence of it is deceptively simple. It is a means whereby the soul can withdraw from the mundane world and engage with the Divine reality that sustains all things. Underpinning this discipline is a principle that is also to be seen in the practice of *Lectio Divina*, a method of prayer

---

[12] John Climacus, ca. 580–650. Abbot of the convent of St. Catherine at the foot of Mt. Sinai, he was given the name Climacus because of his famous spiritual work, *The Ladder* (Greek: *Klimax*), which details a system of spiritual development. The focal point is the invocation of the name of Jesus.

that probably evolved from the same desert wellspring as the Jesus Prayer. This method describes four stages of prayer: *lectio*; *meditatio*; *oratio,* and *contemplatio.* The first, *lectio,* is concerned with prayer recited aloud and repetitively. The second, *meditatio,* is concerned with the methodical process of silently uttering and reflecting upon the nature and significance of the words of the prayer: it is in fact a meditative discipline. The third, *oratio,* is concerned with affective prayer; it is a less discursive engagement with the central theme of the prayer, wherein a more intuitive experience of spiritual reality may occur. The fourth and last is *contemplatio,* which is probably best described as a sublime form of agape wherein the soul rests in the presence of God. Thus it is possible to see that the methodology of this form of prayer is designed to draw the soul out of the world of the senses through the treacherous world of the sphere of sensation and discursive mind into the still waters of the spirit. It is a method that is essentially the same as that used in the Jesus Prayer. John Climacus states that, "The beginning of prayer is the expulsion of distractions from the very start by a single thought (*monologistos*); the middle stage is the concentration on what is being said or thought; its conclusion is rapture in the Lord."[13]

In another work,[14] Ignatius introduces us to the way of using the Jesus Prayer. It is strikingly similar to the methodology of *Lectio Divina.* He instructs us that the words should at first be spoken aloud and without hurry, with the attention focussed entirely upon the words and their significance. He informs us that the mind should be concentrated on one

---

[13] John Climacus, *The Ladder of Divine Ascent: Classics of Western Spirituality* (Mahwah, NJ: Paulist Press, 1982), p. 276.

[14] Ignatius Brainchaninov, *The Arena: An Offering to Contemporary Monasticism,* Archimandrite Lazarus, trans. (Jordanville, NY: Holy Trinity Monastery, 1997), p. 78–79.

single thought, which is embodied in the prayer itself: the thought of our forgiveness by Jesus Christ. When the mind is truly attentive, then the prayer will automatically pass from the "vocal" state to the "mental" state, and then, under the right conditions, it will enter the heart. He warns us that at first the practice of this prayer is dry and uncomfortable, but in due course, if the intention is true, it will become the most fruitful of the soul's endeavours. The Jesus Prayer, he says, is divided into two forms. The first he describes as "vocal" and the second as "mental." At first he recommends that the Jesus Prayer be practised standing upright, breathing gently and with care. He recommends that we should set ourselves the task of saying the prayer one hundred times, unhurried and with complete concentration on its significance. This should take thirty minutes or thereabouts, although some people may take longer. Whatever the circumstances, do not hurry through these prayers; rather, make a short pause between each prayer, reflecting upon its meaning. Then, in due course increase the number to two hundred, then three hundred and so on.

There is a secret to the Jesus Prayer that concerns the heart. When we have examined our conscience, reflecting upon our lives in the context of our prayer, there comes a time when we are able to look deep into our heart, so that eventually our prayer enters into and becomes the rhythm of the heart and we stop thinking with our heads. Herein the nature of the words of the Jesus Prayer become truly meaningful in a way beyond the understanding of the mind; indeed the Jesus Prayer becomes the prayer of the heart itself, then it is possible for us to be forgiven and cleansed, and thus able to abide in the presence of God, His light penetrating every fibre of our being. This is the testimony of those who have trodden the path of the Hesychast.

Those who would know the divine within themselves, Ignatius writes, should purify the heart with unceasing remembrance of God, and that the spiritual land of a pure soul is "within." He says, quoting Isaac the Syrian, that, "The sun which shines in it is the light of the Holy Trinity. The air which its inhabitant breathes is the all-holy spirit. The life, joy and gladness of that country is Christ, the Light of the Light—the Father. That is the Jerusalem or kingdom of God hidden *within us*. . . Try to enter the cell within you, and you will see the heavenly cell. They are one and the same. By one entry you enter both. The ladder to the Heavenly Kingdom is within you. It is built mysteriously in your soul. Immerse yourself within yourself beyond the reach of sin, and you will find there steps by which you can mount to heaven."[15]

Bishop Ignatius Brianchaninov's book is a valuable aid for anyone seeking spiritual knowledge, but it is particularly valuable for those who are treading the path of the Western Mystery Tradition. For those who are prepared to read between the lines, this book represents a rare insight to the greatest mystery of all—the Soul.

Allan Armstrong
Prior of the
Order of Dionysis & Paul
February 2006

[15] St. Isaac the Syrian, chapter 8, quoted in Ignatius Brianchaninov, *On the Prayer of Jesus* (Berwick, ME: Ibis Press, 2006), p. 40.

PREFACE

This translation was begun from the 1865 edition. On reaching page 342 it was discovered that pages 343-346 were missing. A search on the Mount of Olives for another copy of Brianchaninov's book was at last rewarded, but the second copy proved to be a different edition (1905) containing numerous lengthy amplifications. Most of the changes in the later edition have now been incorporated in the present translation.

As far as possible the passages from the *Philokalia* have been translated from the original Greek. In a few cases, particularly where the context required it, Brianchaninov's version has been rendered literally.

The Septuagint, which was the version of Holy Scripture used by our Saviour and the Apostles and for a thousand years by the whole Christian Church, is still the Orthodox Church's authoritative version of the Old Testament. All the quotations in this book are taken from the Slavonic translation of the Septuagint. In checking the Old Testament references it is therefore necessary to bear in mind that there are books and chapter divisions of the Septuagint and Vulgate that differ from those of the Hebrew version. So in order to find the passages cited, the reader should use a Septuagint, Vulgate, Slavonic, Russian or Douai version. The various Protestant translations made from the Hebrew text will frequently be found disappointing. To take a single example, how different is the Septuagint version of Joshua 4: 24! It reads: "That all the nations of the earth might know that the power of the Lord is great, and that you may worship the Lord our God by everything that you do."

TRANSLATOR.

INTRODUCTION

In the early nineteenth century Ignatii Brianchaninov, a Bishop of the Russian Orthodox Church, wrote several essays on Asceticism. One of these essays, dealing with the spiritual exercise based on the Jesus Prayer, and called Hesychasm, has in this work been translated by the Very Reverend Archimandrite Lazarus.

Hesychasm gives expression to the method of enlightenment which has been in use in Christian monasteries in the East almost from Apostolic times. It was given final expression by St. Gregory Palamas sometime in the fourteenth century.

All the ascetic writings on the Jesus Prayer are founded on religious instructions contained in the " Philokalia " (a Greek word meaning " Love of Beauty " or " Love of the Good "). The five volumes of this book, which have been preserved in the monasteries of Mount Athos, contain a collection of precepts and other writings of Christian Fathers from the fourth to the fourteenth century. The collection, beginning with the four books of St. Antony, who died in A.D. 356, and ending with the Work on Asceticism of St. Gregory Palamas, who died in 1360, thus embraces a thousand years of Christian thought expounded by some thirty-five Church Fathers.

The practice of Hesychasm falls into three parts : first the prayer is repeated orally a specified number of times each day " in silence and in solitude," then it is repeated silently in the mind an increased number of times during the day or night, and finally it is carried down into the heart using the rhythm of the heart beats.

It is then carried on incessantly so that the Apostle Paul's injunction, " Pray without ceasing " (1 Thess. 5 : 17) is fulfilled. Or again we are acting according to the charge, " By Him, therefore let us offer a sacrifice of praise to God continually, that is the fruit of our lips giving thanks to His Name " (Heb. 13 : 15). Thirdly, King David reminds us, " I behold the Lord always before me " (Ps. 15 : 8). Other reminders are given in Rom. 12 : 12 and Col. 4 : 2.

This way of praying is not only different, but has a different objective from that of the accepted idea of prayer. Through the ages man has prayed, but he has looked upon prayer as a means of obtaining, generally for himself, something which he wanted. Prayer is, to the average man, asking for something.

However quiescent the Jesus Prayer may seem, it is, in reality, an intensely active process and is a scientific attempt to change the one who prays.

The Jesus Prayer is first repeated aloud again and again. This may be looked upon as the conditioning of the body. It is to gain an external habit of saying the prayer, to make the prayer a continuous background to one's life.

When this has been practised for some time the next step is taken, which is to say the prayer silently, and this might be looked upon as the conditioning of the mind. The prayer must no longer be repeated by the lips but must be concentrated on as it is being thought. Again and again the mind must be brought back to the prayer until one realises that the mind is indeed like " a wagon load of monkeys."

The third step, when complete concentration has been attained, is then taken. The direct link is created between body and spirit and the "divine intermediary" [of] the soul is dispensed with. Now the prayer enters the heart and lives ITSELF with every heart beat (Rom. 8: 26).

Of course it may be argued that man has only a proto-type soul, only a possibility of developing a Spirit. Theologically man can, at best, only reflect God. That may well be. I am inclined to think that this is all only intellectual speculation, and "profiteth nothing" but vanity. In any case the various arguments put forward still hold good.

When the Jesus Prayer is used in this way the disciple changes himself, remakes himself and becomes a totally different person. As St. Paul says; "Put on the new man."

It is in effect a system of self-training, a stern discipline which the disciple deliberately undertakes in order to fit himself for communion with God.

As can readily be seen, this method of prayer differs entirely from that which is normally used and which always consists in asking for something.

Recently the Western world has had an opportunity of learning a great deal about the Jesus Prayer from several books, notably from "The Way of a Pilgrim" published by S.P.C.K., and also by Sheed & Ward in "A Treasury of Russian Spirituality," which explains the theoretical and practical sides of Hesychasm.

When Byzantium fell it was Moscow that became the third Rome and inherited all the Byzantine traditions; amongst these was the protection of the Orthodox religion in the Near East. The Russian monks started visiting the monasteries on Mount Athos which led to the adoption in practice of the precepts of the Philokalia in Russia.

Although this form of inner prayer was first developed for monks who had renounced the world, there were later, nevertheless, certain religious authorities who advised this practice also for the layman. But all were agreed on one point, that at no time should this form of prayer be attempted unless under the direction of a spiritual teacher who would understand all the temptations and dangers which might beset the novice on his religious path.

Among the recent books dealing with the spiritual development of man, is one written by J. G. Bennett, "The Crisis in Human Affairs" in which the author stresses the necessity of "schools" for those who desire to be awakened. It was in this way that the early monasteries were used. The monks had a common aim and, living together, had a common spiritual director to whom they looked for advice and instruction. The straight and narrow path is a very thorny one and is often hard to see without proper guidance.

There are no short cuts. As a pool when vigorously stirred becomes muddy before the dirt subsides and the water becomes crystal clear, so the inner psyche of man becomes turbulant and even violent when stirred by such a deeply religious exercise as Hesychasm. If this work be properly and conscientiously carried out, man becomes aware of all his inner shortcomings and of the dark corners of his soul. Moreover, it seems to him, at least for a time, that all his outward life goes awry. This is the moment when the help of a spiritual director is indispensable; otherwise the aspirant may ascribe to the practice of the Jesus Prayer all his newly arisen bodily and mental ills and may thus become deranged in his mind, growing more unbalanced as he progresses. As St. Paul says "Now we see through a glass darkly . . ." only the glass can become darker still before we see "face to face."

Many people are incapable of believing that a mere repetition, even of a prayer, can lead to any spiritual result. "Why," they say, "should a kind of mumbo-jumbo awake the inner psyche of man?" This point can be argued from several angles, using different vocabularies, depending on the particular prejudices and points of view of the individual.

Put into non-theological language it may well be that the Jesus Prayer acts as a constant reminder to make man look inwards AT ALL TIMES, to become aware of his fleeting thoughts, sudden emotions and even movements so that it may make him try to control them. This self-study and these attempts at self-control lead to an inner friction and man grows in spirituality through that "internal warmth" mentioned by the Fathers in the "Philokalia."

The most necessary quality which should be cultivated by the aspirant is that of humility.

A man deluding himself that he has "will" (instead of a certain freedom of choice) and that he has everything under control, may decide to repeat the Jesus Prayer as a conscious invocation, say three thousand times. He starts, and before very long will, inevitably, find that his thoughts or emotions have taken control and that he is not in fact repeating the prayer. He starts again, and again this happens. Or it may be that he finds himself merely repeating the words of the prayer as a kind of sing-song and his thoughts are elsewhere. If he is honest with himself he will see that he has no control over his thoughts or his emotions or even over his movements: that he has, in fact, no "will," and from this he will learn humility.

By scrutinising and observing his own inner self he will obtain an increasing knowledge of his worthlessness which may fill him with despair. He may then not have enough faith to believe that the Grace of God, at that precise moment, can and will help him to get clear of the morass of passions and bodily stirrings. These are the birth pangs of the spirit and the groanings of awakening spirituality in man.

One is advised to repeat the prayer of Jesus in "silence and solitude."

Silence here is meant to include inner silence; the silence of one's own mind, the arresting of the imagination from the ever-turbulent and ever-present stream of thoughts, words, impressions, pictures and day-dreams, which keep one asleep. This is not easy, as the mind works almost autonomously, much in the same way as do the digestive contractions of one's intestines, of which one is not even aware.

Solitude may mean many things. It certainly means, a phase at least, of physical solitude. But it also implies the solitude of one's soul, the elimination of all ordinary human frailties, of human weaknesses. The awful solitude of the Self.

Little by little the disciple will learn to watch the thoughts which interrupt his inner prayer and will achieve a degree of self-knowledge that may reveal to him many details of the inner mechanism of his own psyche. These will not be the imaginary fantasies with which a man usually solaces himself.

In one of the early "Patrologia" we read that an elderly monk "allowed the thought to come to him that he should go and visit a Father who lived in the desert." The "he allowed the thought to come to him" shows the degree of spiritual control and awareness he had achieved.

Another point of view can be put in this way:— man is a trinity of energies, which may be called spirit, soul and body; of these the soul may be regarded as a vehicle for the spirit in the body. By repeating the Jesus Prayer with "warmth of feeling" and conscientious fervour, man touches that part of himself which is created in the image and likeness of God and learns how he, himself, can become a Son of God.

However, many will prefer to believe that "He who has made us," if implored long enough and with sufficient desire and stability of purpose, may be moved to take compassion on us and save us, if we strive to make ourselves worth saving.

It is generally agreed that our modern world, although it has achieved much in the way of progress, has also lost a great deal of spiritual strength: the morals and the principles of people are at a very low ebb. The mere fact that such amoral movements as fascism and communism have occurred at all in this century shows this loss of spirituality amongst civilised people. Our highly organised material civilisation without a correspondingly high level of spiritual development is indeed a "house built on shifting sands" and as a result we are all unbalanced and unstable.

A great deal has been written and preached on this subject but very little, if any, impression has been made on people in general. I believe that the spirit can only be strengthened through greater self-knowledge on the part of every individual, otherwise the blind will still be leading the blind towards utter chaos and our cycle of civilisation will crumble into dust. Plato said of the prisoners in the cave who could only see the shadows of reality outside and to whom these shadows were in fact actual existence, should they have managed to get away from their shackles and walk out of the cave into the full sunlight of reality, they would not even have had any words to describe it. This, I think, is about the best illustration of the position in which human beings find themselves, bound as they are to their senses and their fantasies.

There are, however, people who are searching, groping in the darkness towards the light. Even "trying to see" is a step in the right direction. This book shows one way to greater awareness. Each man must, to start with, try to open his own eyes before he can do anything for his fellow-men, no matter what the nature of the ultimate truth may be. These ancient writings may awaken some people to their spiritual needs, help them to have more knowledge of themselves and lead them to a different state of consciousness.

While some parts of Bishop Brianchaninov's book requre a great deal of understanding and knowledge on the part of the serious student, other parts give such a clear and simple exposition of certain spiritual truths that they can be readily assimilated by anyone who wishes to grow in spirituality, so there is ample food for both the initiated and the beginner.

It also seems to me that the literature of the West should possess a record of this ancient form of spiritual endeavour, preserved in the East by the Grace of the All Merciful God. It is here ably and sympathetically rendered into modern English by Father Lazarus, whom, I hope I am privileged to call my friend.

My thanks are due to Nathanael, Bishop of Preston and the Hague, and to Mrs. Stanley Wood for reading this manuscript and giving me many valuable suggestions and making corrections.

If the reader should be interested in further study of the

Early Christian Fathers mentioned by Bishop Brianchaninov, I would refer him to "Writings from the Philokalia," translated by E. Kadloubovsky and G. E. Palmer, published by Faber & Faber.

Another important addition to the literature on Inner Prayer has just been published by Faber & Faber entitled "Unseen Warfare," being the Spiritual Combat and Path to Paradise of Lorenzo Scupoli as edited by Nicodemus of the Holy Mountain and revised by Theophan the Recluse, translated by E. Kadloubovsky and G. E. Palmer. More important still is the reasoned and scholarly introduction to this work by Professor H. A. Hodges of Reading University, which explains clearly the many processes which compose the entire practice of Hesychasm, it is itself a valuable contribution to the study of this Eastern Orthodox theme.

ALEXANDER d'AGAPEYEFF.

Maugersbury Manor,
Gloucestershire.

ON THE
PRAYER OF JESUS

In beginning to speak of the prayer of Jesus, I invoke the aid of the all-good and almighty Jesus that He may assist my dullness. In beginning to speak of the prayer of Jesus, I recall the righteous Simeon's utterance concerning the Lord: *Behold, this One is destined for the fall and rising of many in Israel, and for a sign that is spoken against* (Lk. 2: 34). Just as the Lord was and is a true sign, a sign that is spoken against, an object of dispute and disagreement between those who know Him and those who do not, so too prayer in His all-holy name, which in the fullest sense is a great and wonderful sign, has become a subject of dispute and disagreement between those who practise it and those who do not. A certain Father justly remarks that this way of prayer is rejected only by those who do not know it; they reject it through prejudice and through false ideas that they have formed of it.

Without paying any attention to the outcries of prejudice and ignorance, trusting in the mercy and help of God, we offer beloved fathers and brothers our poor treatise (lit. word) on the prayer of Jesus on the basis of Holy Scripture, on the basis of Church tradition, on the basis of the writings of the Fathers in which the teaching of this all-holy and all-powerful prayer is expounded. *Let lying lips be dumb which speak iniquity against* His *just* and magnificent name *in their pride,* in their profound ignorance *and abuse* of God's wonders. As we consider the greatness of the name of Jesus and the saving power of prayer in that name, we cry with spiritual joy and amazement: *How great is the multitude of Thy goodness, O Lord, which Thou hast hidden for them that fear Thee, which Thou hast wrought for them that hope in Thee before the sons of men* (Ps. 30: 19-20).

The prayer of Jesus is said like this: *Lord Jesus Christ, Son of God, have mercy on me a sinner.* Originally it was said without the addition of the word *sinner*: this word was added to the other words of the prayer later. This word, remarks St. Nile[1] Sorsky, which implies a consciousness and confession of the fall, is fitting for us and pleasing to God Who has commanded us to offer prayers in acknowledgment and confession of our sinfulness.[2] The Fathers allow beginners, in deference to their weakness, to divide the prayer into two halves, and sometimes to say, *Lord Jesus Christ, have mercy on me a sinner*, and sometimes, *Son of God, have mercy on me a sinner.* But this is only a concession or indulgence, and not at all an order or rule requiring unfailing compliance. It is much better to say constantly the same, whole prayer without distracting and bothering the mind with changes or with concern about changes. Even he who finds a change necessary for his weakness should not allow it often. For example, the first half of the prayer can be prayed till dinner, and the other after dinner. St. Gregory the Sinaite forbids frequent change, saying: "Trees that are often transplanted do not take root."

Praying by the prayer of Jesus is a divine institution. It was instituted not by means of an Apostle or by means of an Angel; it was instituted by the Son of God and God

---

[1] The "i" in Nile is pronounced as in *machine*.
[2] St. Nile Sorsky, Ch. 2.

Himself. After the mystical supper among other sublime, final commandments and orders, the Lord Jesus Christ instituted prayer by His name. He gave this way of prayer as a new, extraordinary gift, a gift of infinite value. The Apostles partly knew already the power of the name of Jesus; they healed incurable diseases by it, they reduced devils to obedience, conquered, bound and expelled them by it. This most mighty, wonderful name the Lord orders us to use in prayer. He promised that such prayer will be particularly effectual. *Whatever you ask,* He said to the holy Apostles, *the Father in My name, I will do, that the Father may be glorified in the Son. If you ask anything in My name, I will do it* (Jn. 14: 13). *Truly, truly, I tell you, if you ask anything of the Father in My name, He will give it you. Till now you have asked nothing in My name; ask and you will receive, that your joy may be full* (Jn. 15: 23).

What a wonderful gift! It is a guarantee of unending, infinite blessings! It came from the lips of the unlimited God, clothed in limited humanity and called by the human name of Saviour.[1] The name by its exterior form is limited, but it represents an unlimited object, God, from Whom it borrows infinite, divine value or worth, the power and properties of God.

O Giver of a priceless, incorruptible gift! How can we sinful mortals receive the gift? Neither our hands, nor our mind, nor our heart are capable of receiving it. Do Thou teach us to know, as far as we are able, the greatness of the gift, and its significance, and the ways of receiving it, and the ways of using it, that we may not approach the gift in a sinful manner, that we may not be punished for indiscretion and audacity, but that for the right understand-

---

[1] Saviour—in Hebrew, *Jesus* (Matt. 1: 21).

ing and use of the gift, we may receive from Thee other gifts, promised by Thee, known only to Thee.

From the Gospels, the Acts and the Apostolic Epistles we see the unbounded faith of the holy Apostles in the name of the Lord Jesus and their unbounded reverence for this name. By the name of the Lord Jesus they performed the most striking miracles. There is no instance from which we can learn how they prayed in the name of the Lord. But that is certainly how they prayed. How could they do otherwise when that prayer was given and commanded them by the Lord Himself, and when the order was confirmed by a twofold repetition of it? If Scripture is silent about it, it is silent only because this prayer was in general use and was so well known that it needed no special mention in Scripture. Even in the monuments of the first ages of Christianity that have come down to us, prayer in the name of the Lord is not treated separately but is only mentioned in connection with other matters.

In the life of St. Ignatius the God-bearer, Bishop of Antioch, who was crowned in Rome with a martyr's death under the emperor Trajan, we read the following: "When they were taking him to be devoured by wild beasts and he had the name of Jesus constantly on his lips, the pagans asked him why he unceasingly remembered that name. The Saint replied that he had the name of Jesus Christ written in his heart and that he confessed with his mouth Him Whom he always carried in his heart. After the Saint had been eaten by the wild beasts, by the will of God among his bones his heart was preserved intact. The infidels found it, and then remembered what St. Ignatius had said. So they cut that heart into two halves, wishing to know whether what they had been told was true. Inside, on the two halves of the heart that had been cut open, they found an inscription in gold letters: *Jesus Christ*. Thus St. Ignatius was in name and in fact a God-bearer, always carrying Christ our God in his heart, written by the reflection (or meditation) of his mind as with a reed."

St. Ignatius was a disciple of the holy Apostle and Evangelist John the Divine, and was privileged in his childhood to see the Lord Jesus Christ personally. He was that blessed child of whom it is said in the Gospel that the Lord placed him among the Apostles who had been arguing about priority, took him in His arms and said: *Truly I tell you, unless you turn and become like children, you will never enter the Kingdom of Heaven. For whoever humbles himself like a child, he is the greatest in the Kingdom of Heaven.*[1]

Certainly St. Ignatius was taught the prayer of Jesus by the holy Evangelist and practised it in that flourishing period of Christianity like all other Christians. At that time all Christians learnt the prayer of Jesus, firstly on account of the great importance of the prayer itself, and then on account of the scarcity and costliness of the handwritten holy books, on account of the rarity of literacy (most of the Apostles were illiterate), and on account of the convenience, satisfaction and very special action and power of the prayer of Jesus.

In Church History we read the following incident: "A soldier called Neokorus, a native of Carthage, was in the Roman garrison guarding Jerusalem at the time when our Lord Jesus Christ suffered His voluntary passion and death for the redemption of the human race. Seeing the miracles worked at the Lord's death and resurrection, Neokorus

---

[1] Matt. 18 : 3-4. Cp. Mk. 9 : 36, and Menology for Dec. 20.

believed in the Lord and was baptized by the Apostles.
After finishing his term of service, Neokorus returned to
Carthage and shared the treasure of faith with his whole
family. Among those who accepted Christianity was
Callistratus, Neokorus' grandson. On reaching the required
age, Callistratus joined the army. The detachment of
soldiers to which he was drafted consisted of idolaters.
They watched Callistratus and noticed that he did not worship the idols but spent a long time in prayer at night alone.
Once they eavesdropped while he was praying and heard
that he constantly repeated the name of the Lord Jesus
Christ. So they reported him to the commanding officer.
Saint Callistratus who confessed Jesus alone in the dark
at night also confessed Him publicly in the light of day, and
sealed his confession with his blood."[1]

Teaching on the prayer of Jesus appears in Church
writers of the fourth century such as John Chrysostom and
Isaiah the Solitary. A writer of the fifth century, St.
Hesychius of Jerusalem, already complains that the practice of
this prayer has greatly declined among monks. As time went
on, this decline increased more and more. So the holy
Fathers tried by their writings to encourage the practice.
The last writer on this prayer was the blessed elder,
hieromonk Seraphim of Sarov.[2] The elder himself did not
write the instructions bearing his name; they were written
down from his words by one of the monks under his direction, but they are written with remarkable unction. Now
the practice of the prayer of Jesus has been almost
abandoned by monks and nuns. St. Hesychius names care-

---

[1] Menology, Sept. 27th.

[2] Brianchaninov wrote half a century before St. Seraphim's
canonisation.

lessness as the cause of this neglect. It must be admitted that this accusation is just.

The gracious power of the prayer of Jesus is contained in the divine name itself of the God-man, our Lord Jesus Christ. Although there is abundant evidence in Holy Scripture proving the greatness of the name of God, yet the importance of this name was explained with special precision by the holy Apostle Peter before the Jewish sanhedrin, when the council asked the Apostle *by what power or by what name* he had given healing to a man lame from birth. *Peter, filled with the Holy Spirit, said: Rulers of the people and elders of Israel, if we are being examined today concerning a good deed done to a cripple, by what means this man has been healed, be it known to you all, and to all the people of Israel that by the name of Jesus Christ of Nazareth, Whom you crucified, Whom God raised from the dead, by Him this man is standing before you well. This is the stone which was rejected by you builders, but which has become the head of the corner. And there is salvation in no one else, for there is no other name under heaven given among men by which we must be saved* (Acts 4: 8-12). This witness is the testimony of the Holy Spirit. The Apostle's mouth, tongue, and voice were merely the Spirit's instruments.

Another organ of the Holy Spirit, the Apostle of the Gentiles, gives similar evidence. *Everyone,* he says, *who calls upon the name of the Lord will be saved* (Rom. 10: 13). *Christ Jesus . . . humbled Himself and became obedient till death, even to death on a cross. Therefore God has highly exalted Him and given Him the name that is above every name, that in the name of Jesus every knee should bow, in heaven and on earth and under the earth* (Phil. 2: 5-10).

Seeing the distant future, David, an ancestor of Jesus according to the flesh, sang the greatness of the name of Jesus, and vividly described the effect of this name, the struggle by means of it with the principles of sin, its power to deliver those who pray by it from captivity to the passions and demons, and the triumph of those who win a spiritual victory by the name of Jesus. Let us listen to inspired David! *O Lord our Lord*, he cries, *how wonderful is Thy name in all the earth! For Thy magnificence is raised above the heavens. Out of the mouth of babes and sucklings Thou hast perfected praise, because of Thy enemies, that Thou mayst destroy the enemy and avenger* (Ps. 8: 2). Exactly! The greatness of the name of Jesus is beyond the comprehension of rational creatures of earth and heaven. The comprehension of it is incomprehensibly grasped by child-like simplicity and faith. In this same disinterested spirit we must approach prayer in the name of Jesus and continue in that prayer. Our perseverance and attention in prayer must be like the constant striving of an infant for its mother's breasts. Then prayer in the name of Jesus will be crowned with complete success, the invisible foes will be defeated, and *the enemy and avenger* will be finally crushed. The *enemy* is called *the avenger* because he tries to take from those who pray (especially at times, not incessantly) after prayer what they have obtained during prayer. In order to win a decisive victory unceasing prayer and constant vigilance are indispensable.

OPEN TO ALL.

On account of the importance of prayer in the name of Jesus, David invites all Christians to the practice of this prayer. *Praise the Lord, ye children, praise the name of the Lord. Blessed be the name of the Lord, from now and for ever. From sunrise till sunset His name is worthy of praise* (Ps. 112: 1-3). *Offer to the Lord glory to His name, worship the Lord in His holy court* (Ps. 28: 2). Pray in this way so that in your prayers the greatness of the name of Jesus may be manifested and by its power you may rise to the inner temple not made with hands (the temple of the heart) and worship in spirit and truth. Pray carefully and constantly. Pray in fear and trembling before the greatness of the name of Jesus, *and let them trust in Thee,* the almighty and all-good Jesus, *who know Thy name* from their own blessed experience, *for Thou hast never forsaken them that seek Thee, O Lord* (Ps. 9: 11).

Only the poor in spirit who cling constantly to the Lord by prayer on account of the constant sense of their poverty and need are capable of discovering within themselves the greatness of the name of Jesus. *Let not the humble man be put to confusion* and disappointed in his prayer, but let him offer it to God whole, not torn by distraction. *The poor and needy shall praise Thy name* (Ps. 73: 21). *Blessed is the man whose trust is in the name of the Lord, and who has not had regard to vanities and lying follies* (Ps. 39: 5). He will not pay any attention during his prayer to the seductive action of vain cares and passions˙which attempt to defile and spoil his prayer.

Night-time is particularly helpful for the practice of the prayer of Jesus on account of the darkness and silence. At night that great man of prayer, David, occupied himself with the remembrance of God: *I have remembered Thy name, O Lord, in the night,* he says. I tuned my soul at night to a divine pitch, *and,* having acquired that pitch in the activity of the following day *I have kept Thy law* (Ps. 118: 55). "At night," advises St. Gregory the Sinaite, quoting St. John of the Ladder, "devote much time to prayer, and little to psalmody."

In the grim struggle with the invisible enemies of our salvation, the supreme weapon is the prayer of Jesus. *All the nations*—the vociferous and wily demons are called nations—*surrounded me*, says David *and in the name of the Lord I repulsed them. They encircled and surrounded me, and in the name of the Lord I repulsed them. They surrounded me like bees, and they burnt like fire among thorns; and in the name of the Lord I repulsed them* (Ps. 117: 10-12). "With the name of Jesus flog the foes, because there is no stronger weapon in heaven or earth."[1] *Through Thee, Lord Jesus, we will push down our enemies with the horn, and through Thy name we will despise them that rise up against us. For I will not trust in my bow, neither will my sword save me. But Thou hast saved us from them that afflict us, and Thou hast put to shame them that hate us. In God shall we glory all the day long, and in Thy name we will give thanks for ever* (Ps. 43: 6-9).

Having conquered and dispersed the enemies by the name of Jesus, the mind joins the ranks of the blessed spirits and enters for true worship into the temple of the heart which had previously been closed to it, singing a new, spiritual song, singing mystically: *I will thank Thee, O Lord, with my whole heart, I will praise Thee before the Angels, for Thou hast heard all the words of my mouth. I will worship towards Thy holy temple, and I will give thanks to Thy name for Thy mercy and for Thy truth: for Thou hast magnified Thy holy name above all. In whatever day I call upon*

---

[1] Ladder of Paradise : 21, 7.

Thee, speedily hear me; Thou wilt multiply Thy strength in my soul (Ps. 137: 1-3).

Saint David enumerates the wonderful effects of the *holy and terrible name* of Jesus (Ps. 110: 9). It acts like a medicine whose way of acting is unknown and incomprehensible to the patient but whose effect is obvious from the healing produced. For the sake of the name of Jesus used by one who prays, help comes down to him from God and he is granted the forgiveness of his sins. For this reason holy David, presenting to the gaze of God the forlorn and wretched state of the soul of every man produced by a sinful life, prays in the person of all men for mercy, saying: *Help us, O God, our Saviour; and for the glory of Thy name, O Lord, deliver us; and forgive us our sins for Thy name's sake* (Ps. 78: 9). For the sake of the Lord's name our prayer is heard and we are granted salvation. On the basis of this conviction again David prays: *Save me, O God, by Thy name, and judge me by Thy power. O God, hear my prayer; attend to the words of my mouth* (Ps. 53: 3).

By the power of the name of Jesus the mind is freed from doubt, indecision and hesitation, the will is strengthened and correctness is given to zeal and other properties of the soul. Then only thoughts and feelings pleasing to God, thoughts and feelings belonging to undepraved human nature, only such thoughts and feelings are allowed to remain in the soul. There is no place then for other thoughts and feelings, *for God will save Sion and the cities of Judah will be built; and men will dwell there, and inherit it. And the seed of Thy slaves will possess it; and they who love Thy name will dwell in it* (Ps. 68: 36). In the name of the Lord Jesus quickening is given to the soul deadened by sin. The Lord Jesus Christ is life. And His name is living; it revives and

quickens those who cry by it to the source of life, the Lord
Jesus Christ. *For Thy name's sake, O Lord, Thou wilt
quicken me in Thy righteousness* (Ps. 142: 11). *We shall
not depart from Thee. Thou wilt quicken us, and we will
call upon Thy name* (Ps. 79: 19).

When by the power and action of the name of Jesus a
man's prayer is heard, when divine assistance comes down
to him, when his enemies are defeated and leave him in
peace, when he is granted the forgiveness of his sins, when he
is healed and restored to the state of unsullied nature, when
his spirit comes into its own authority—then follows the
giving of spiritual gifts in the name of the Lord, spiritual
goods and treasure, a pledge of blessed eternity. *For Thou,
O God, hast heard my prayer; Thou hast given an inheritance to them that fear Thy name. Thou wilt add days to
the days of the king, his years till the day of eternity. He
shall continue for ever in the presence of God* (Ps. 60: 6).
Then a man becomes able to *sing to the Lord a new song.*
He ceases to be of the number of the carnal and natural,
and joins the ranks of the spiritual with whom he praises the
Lord *in the church of the saints* (Ps. 149: 1).

The Holy Spirit, Who has hitherto invited and urged him
only to weeping and penitence, now invites him to rejoice:
*Let Israel rejoice in Him Who made him, and let the
children of Sion exult over their King. Let them praise His
name in choir, let them sing to Him with the timbrel and
psaltery* (Ps. 149: 2). That is because, after the soul's
renewal, its powers are brought into wonderful accord and
harmony, and at the touch of divine grace become capable
of producing spiritual sounds and tunes pleasing to God
which rise to heaven before the throne of God. *Let my
heart rejoice to fear Thy name! I will confess Thee, O*

Lord my God, with my whole heart, and I will glorify Thy name for ever; for Thy mercy is great towards me, and Thou hast delivered my soul out of the depths of hell (Ps. 85: 11-13). *The just shall confess Thy name, and the upright shall dwell in Thy presence*[1] (Ps. 139: 14). That is because, after the repulsion of the enemies which cause distraction and weaken and defile prayer, the mind enters the darkness of the unseen and stands in the presence of God without any means or intermediary. This spiritual darkness is that veil, that curtain, which hides the face of God. That veil is the incomprehensibility of God for all created minds. Compunction of heart then becomes so powerful that it is called confession. The blessed effect of the prayer of Jesus in a proficient Christian, David depicts thus: *Bless the Lord, O my soul, and all that is within me bless His holy name* (Ps. 102: 1). EXACTLY! At the abundant action of the prayer of Jesus all the powers of the soul, and even the body, take part in it.

The practice of the prayer of Jesus holy David, or more accurately the Holy Spirit by the mouth of David, offers to all Christians without exception: *The kings of the earth and all people, princes and all judges of the earth, young men and maidens,—let elders with the young praise the name of the Lord, for His name alone is exalted* (Ps. 148: 11-13). A literal understanding of the states enumerated here would be perfectly permissible, but their essential meaning is spiritual. By *people* is meant all Christians: by *kings* is meant Christians who have been granted to attain perfection; by *princes* those who have made very considerable progress; by *judges* is meant those who have not yet acquired authority over themselves, but being acquainted with the Law of God

---

[1] *In Thy presence* : Lit. "with Thy face."

they can distinguish good from evil, and by the guidance and requirement of the Law of God they can continue in good and reject evil. *Maiden* denotes all the female sex and the detached heart which is so apt for prayer. *Elders and the young* indicate degrees of bodily growth and degrees of active progress which is very different from grace-given progress, though the former has its very real value; he who has reached perfection in active prayer is called an *elder*, while he who has been raised to grace-given perfection is a *king*.

POWER TO EXPEL DEMONS.

Among the mysterious, wonderful properties of the name of Jesus is the power and property of expelling demons. This property was disclosed by the Lord Himself. He said that those who believe in Him, *in His name they will cast out demons* (Mk. 16: 17). Special attention must be paid to this property of the name of Jesus, because it is of the greatest importance for those practising the prayer of Jesus. First of all a few words must be said concerning the dwelling of demons in human beings. This occurs in two ways: one can be called sensible, the other moral. Satan dwells sensibly in a man when with his being he occupies the man's body, and tortures body and soul. In this way it is possible for one devil to live in a man, and it is also possible for many devils to live in the same man. Then a man is called possessed or a demoniac. From the Gospel we see that our Lord healed people possessed with devils. The Lord's disciples also healed them; they expelled demons from people by the name of the Lord.

Satan dwells morally in a man when the man becomes a doer of the devil's will. It was in this way that *satan entered* into Judas Iscariot (Jn. 13: 27), that is, he controlled his reason and will, and became one with him in spirit. All non-believers in Christ were and are in this state, as the holy Apostle Paul says to Christians who had been converted to Christianity from paganism: *And you He made alive, when you were dead through your trespasses and sins in which you once walked, following the course of this world, following the prince of the power of the air, the spirit that is now at work in the sons of disobedience. Among these we all once lived in the passions of our flesh, following the desires of the flesh and the mind, and so we were by nature children of wrath, like the rest of mankind* (Ephes. 2: 1-3). In this state more or less, according to the degree of their sinfulness, are those who have been baptized into Christ but who have become estranged from Him by sin. That is how the holy Fathers understand Christ's words regarding the return of the devil with seven other more evil spirits to the temple of the soul from which it had been expelled by the Holy Spirit.[1] When spirits enter in this way, they can be driven out again by the prayer of Jesus, accompanied by a life of constant and diligent penitence.

Let us take up this neglected work so directly concerned with our salvation! Let us do all in our power to expel demons that have entered us through our negligence by the prayer of Jesus. It has the property of reviving those deadened by sin, and it has the property of driving out devils. *I am the resurrection and the life,* said the Saviour. *He who believes in Me, even though he dies, will live* (Jn. 11: 25). *These signs will accompany those who believe:*

---

[1] Matt. 12 : 43-45.

in My name they will cast out demons (Mk. 16: 17). The
prayer of Jesus both reveals the presence of demons in a
man, and drives them out of the man. Herein is accomplished something like what took place when the Lord
expelled the demon from the possessed boy after His transfiguration. When the lad saw the Lord coming, *the spirit
convulsed the boy, and he fell on the ground and rolled about,
foaming at the mouth* (Mk. 9: 20). When the Lord commanded the evil spirit to leave its victim, out of malice and
wickedness as it came out it shrieked out and violently convulsed the boy so that it seemed as if he were dead.

The power of satan, which dwells in a man as a result
of his dissolute life unnoticed and unrealised, when it hears
the name of the Lord Jesus invoked in prayer, becomes
agitated and confused. It stirs up all the passions and by
this means reduces the whole man to a terrible state of
agitation and produces in the body various strange maladies.
It was in this connection that St. John the Prophet said: "It
only remains for us weak creatures to have recourse to the
name of Jesus, for the passions are demons and depart at
the invocation of this name." That means that the action
of the passions and demons is a combined action; the
demons act by means of the passions. When we see a
special disturbance and excitement of the passions accom-
panying the prayer of Jesus, let us not be dejected or per-
plexed by it. On the contrary, let us take courage and prepare ourselves for the struggle and for the most diligent
prayer in the name of Jesus as having received a clear sign
that the prayer of Jesus has begun to produce its proper
effect in us.

St. John Chrysostom says: "The remembrance of the
name of Jesus rouses the enemy to battle. For a soul that

forces itself to pray the prayer of Jesus can find anything by this prayer, both good and evil. First it can see evil in the recesses of its own heart, and afterwards good. This prayer can stir the snake to action, and this prayer can lay it low. This prayer can expose the sin that is living in us, and this prayer can eradicate it. This prayer can stir up in the heart all the power of the enemy, and this prayer can conquer it and gradually root it out. The name of the Lord Jesus Christ, as it descends into the depths of the heart, will subdue the snake which controls its ranges (pastures), and will save and quicken (revive) the soul. Continue constantly in the name of the Lord Jesus that the heart may swallow the Lord and the Lord the heart, and that these two may be one. However, this is not accomplished in a single day, nor in two days, but requires many years and much time. Much time and labour are needed in order to expel the enemy and instate Christ."

Evidently here is described that activity of which St. Makarius the Great speaks and to which he invites people in his 1st Word, with a clear indication as to the weapon of that warfare: "Force your way in, whoever you are, through the thoughts that incessantly rise up within you, to that prisoner of war and slave of sin—your soul—and look to the very bottom of your mind and examine the depth of your thoughts, and you will see nestling and creeping in the inner recesses of your soul the snake (dragon) which killed you by poisoning the vital parts of your soul. The heart is an unfathomable abyss. If you kill that snake, glory in your purity before God. But if not, humble yourself as one who is weak and sinful, and pray to God for diliverance from your secret sins."[1] The same great servant of God

---

[1] S. Makarius, Word 1, Chap. 1 (*not* from the Homilies).

says: "The kingdom of darkness, that is, the evil prince of spirits, having taken man captive at the beginning, enveloped and clothed his soul in the power of darkness. This evil ruler clothed the soul and all its substance with sin. He defiled it all and brought it all into captivity to his kingdom. He did not leave one member of it free from slavery to himself—neither the thoughts, nor the understanding, nor the body; he clothed it all with the purple of darkness. This evil enemy has defiled and disfigured the entire man, soul and body. He has clothed man in 'the old man,' defiled, unclean, *hostile to God, insubmissive to God's law* (Rom. 8: 7). That is, he has clothed him in sin itself, so that man may no longer see as he wishes, but may see passionately, and hear passionately, and have feet prone to evil deeds, hands to commit sin, and a heart inclined to evil thoughts. But let us implore God to put off the old man from us, since He alone can take away sin from us. For those that have taken us captive, and that detain us in their kingdom, are too mighty for us. But He has promised to deliver us from this slavery."[1]

On the basis of these ideas the holy Fathers give to those who pray the prayer of Jesus the following instructions: "Unless the soul suffers greatly over the importunacy[2] of sin, it cannot rejoice abundantly over the goodness of justice. Whoever wishes to purify his heart, let him burn it out continually with the remembrance of the Lord Jesus Christ, making this his one unceasing meditation and work. Those who desire to renounce their old nature must not sometimes pray and sometimes not, but must unceasingly devote themselves to prayer with watchfulness of mind, even when they

---

[1] Hom. 2: 1-2.
[2] So the Slavonic. Gk. Shamelessness.

are outside temples of prayer. Those who intend to purify gold, if even for a short time they allow the fire to go out in the furnace, they produce hardening again in the material that is being purified. Similarly he who sometimes remembers God and sometimes forgets Him ruins by sloth what he thinks to acquire by prayer. It is the part of a virtue-loving man constantly to root out earthliness of heart by the remembrance of God, so that in this way evil may be gradually consumed by the fire of the remembrance of good and the soul may be perfectly restored to its natural brightness with greater glory. Thus by remaining in the heart, the mind prays purely and without delusion,[1] as the same Saint (Diadochus) has said: Prayer is true and free from delusion[1] when the mind keeps watch over the heart at the time that it prays."[2]

Let us not be scared, practisers of the prayer of Jesus, either by winds or waves! By winds I mean diabolic thoughts and imaginings, and by waves the revolt of the passions aroused by thoughts and reveries. From the midst of the most furious storm, with perseverance, courage and weeping you will cry to the Lord Jesus Christ, and He will rebuke the winds and waves. And having learnt from experience the omnipotence of Jesus, we shall render to Him due adoration, saying: *Thou art indeed the Son of God* (Mat. 14: 33).

We are fighting for our salvation. On our victory or defeat depends our eternal destiny. "Then," says St. Symeon the New Theologian (i.e. during the practice of the

---

[1] "Delusion." So the Russian. The Greek can also mean *distraction* or *wandering*.

[2] SS. Kallistus and Ignatius, *Directions to Hesychasts*, ch. 56 (Philokalia).

C

prayer of Jesus), "there is a battle. The evil spirits fight with great confusion and produce by means of the passions a storm and rebellion in the heart; but by the name of the Lord Jesus Christ they are consumed and destroyed like wax by fire. Yet when they are repulsed and retreat from the heart, they do not abandon the struggle, but they disturb the mind from without through the exterior senses. For this reason the mind does not very soon begin to experience calm and quiet within itself; because when the demons have not the power to disturb the mind in its depths, they disturb it from without by phantasies. And therefore it is impossible to be completely free from conflict and not to be attacked by evil spirits. That belongs only to the perfect and to those who are completely detached from everything and whose attention remains constantly in the heart."[1]

At first the practice of the prayer of Jesus appears to be extraordinarily dry and seems to promise no fruit. As the mind strives to unite with the heart, it meets at first with impenetrable darkness and gloom, hardness and deadness of the heart, which is not quickly aroused to sympathy with the mind. This should not cause despondency and cowardice; it is mentioned here since to be forewarned is to be forearmed. The patient and diligent worker will not fail to be satisfied and consoled; he will rejoice at an infinite abundance of spiritual fruits such as he can form no conception of in his carnal and natural state.

There are degrees of the action of the prayer of Jesus. At first it acts only on the mind, leading it into a state of calm and attention. Afterwards it begins to penetrate to the heart, arousing it from the sleep of death and making its revival known by the manifestation within it of feelings of

---

[1] "On the Third Way of Attention" (Philokalia).

compunction and sorrow. As it goes still deeper, it gradually begins to act upon all the members of the soul and body and to expel sin from every part, and everywhere to destory the dominion, influence and poison of the demons. For this reason at the first actions of the prayer of Jesus "there occurs unutterable contrition and unspeakable pain of soul," says St. Gregory the Sinaite. The soul suffers like a sick man or a woman in travail, as Scripture says (Ecclus. 48: 21). *For the Word of God is living and active, and sharper than any two-edged sword, that is Jesus and pierces to the division of soul and spirit, of joints and marrow, and discerning the thoughts and intentions of the heart* (Heb. 4: 12), eradicating sinfulness from all parts of the soul and the body.

When the seventy lesser Apostles, whom the Lord sent on a preaching tour, returned to Him after carrying out their appointed ministry, they told the Lord with joy: *Lord, even the devils are subject to us in Thy name* (Lk. 10: 17). O, how just was that joy! How reasonable it was! For more than five thousand years the devil had ruled over men, making them his slaves and relatives by means of sin. And now he hears the name of Jesus—and is subject to men who have hitherto been subject to him, is bound by those whom he had bound, is trampled on by those whom he had trampled on. In reply to the disciples who were rejoicing over the conquest of the power of the devils over men and the obtaining by men of power over the demons, the Lord said: *Behold, I give you power to tread upon serpents and scorpions, and upon all the power of the enemy, and nothing shall hurt you* (Lk. 10: 19). The power was given, but freedom was reserved to use the power and trample on snakes and scorpions, or to despise the gift and voluntarily be subject to them. Under the name of snakes the holy Fathers understand openly sinful undertakings, and by scorpions they understand things camouflaged with an exterior of innocence and even goodness.

The power given by the Lord to His seventy disciples is given to all Christians (Mk. 16: 17). Use it, Christian! With the name of Jesus cut off their heads, that is the first appearances of sin in our thoughts, fancies and feelings. Destroy within you the devil's rule over you; destroy all his influence over you; acquire spiritual freedom. The foundation for your struggle is the grace of holy baptism; your weapon is prayer in the name of Jesus.

Having given His disciples power to trample on snakes and scorpions, the Lord added: *But yet rejoice not in this, that spirits are subject to you; but rejoice that your names are written in heaven* (Lk. 10: 20). "Rejoice," says Blessed Theophylact, "not so much over the fact that devils are subject to you, as over the fact that your names are written in heaven, not with ink, but by divine grace and the remembrance of God" through the prayer of Jesus. Such is the property of the prayer of Jesus—it leads its practiser from earth to heaven, and places him among the celestial inhabitants. Dwelling with the mind and heart in heaven and in God—that is the chief fruit, that is the end of prayer. The repulsion and defeat of the enemies which oppose the attainment of this end is a secondary matter; it should not deflect to itself all our attention lest the realisation and consideration of victory should give entry to pride and self-confidence and we suffer a crushing defeat through our very victory.

Further on the Gospel relates: *In that hour Jesus rejoiced in spirit and said: I thank Thee, Father, Lord of heaven and earth, that Thou hast hidden these things from the wise and prudent, and hast revealed them to babes. Yes, Father, for such was Thy gracious will.* And turning to the disciples He said: *All things have been delivered to Me by My Father* (Lk. 10: 21). The Lord rejoices with the incomprehensible joy of God at the success of men. He declares that the mysteries of the Christian faith are revealed not to the wise and exalted of the world, but to those who are children as regards civil affairs, such as were the Lord's disciples, taken from among the simple people, unlearned, illiterate. In order to become a disciple of the Lord we must become infants, and with child-like simplicity and love accept His teaching. To those who have become His disciples the Lord explains His most mystical teaching; He reveals that the Son, in spite of His assuming humanity, remains above the comprehension of all rational creatures. Above their comprehension also is His most holy name. With the simplicity and trust of children let us receive the teaching on prayer in the name of Jesus. With the simplicity and trust of children let us approach the practice of this prayer. God Who alone fully knows the secret of it will give it us in a degree accessible to us. Let us give joy to God[1] by our labours and progress in the service which He has taught and commanded us.

GREEK AND RUSSIAN GUIDES.

The prayer of Jesus was in general use among Christians of the first ages, as we have already said. It could not be otherwise. By the name of the Lord Jesus Christ the most striking miracles were performed in the presence of the

---

[1] Or, "Let us gladden God."

whole Christian community, which encouraged the whole of Christian society to cherish faith in the unbounded power of the name of Jesus. Those who were successful understood this power from their own success. Concerning this power, which was developed abundantly among God's saints, St. Barsanouphius the Great writes: "I know one servant of God in our generation, at the present time and in this blessed place, who can even raise the dead in the name of our Lord Jesus Christ, and can drive out demons, and heal incurable diseases, and can do other miracles no less apostolic, as is promised (cp. Jn. 14: 12) by Him who gave him the gift, or more exactly the gifts. Yes, and what is that in comparison with what can be done in the name of Jesus!"[1]

Having miracles before their eyes, the Lord's command in their memory, and flaming love for the Lord in their heart, the faithful of the primitive Church constantly, diligently and with the fiery zeal of Cherubim and Seraphim exercised themselves in prayer by the name of Jesus. Such is the property of love! It constantly remembers the beloved; it unceasingly delights in the name of the beloved; it keeps it in its heart and has it in its mind and on its lips. The name of the Lord is above every name; it is a source of delight, a source of joy, a source of life. It is Spirit. It quickens (vivifies), transforms, purifies, deifies. For the illiterate it can replace in a completely satisfactory manner vocal prayer and psalmody. The literate, having made some progress in the prayer of Jesus, give up the variety of psalmody and begin pre-eminently to practise the prayer of Jesus on account of the superabundant power and nourishment contained in it. All this is apparent from the

---

[1] Answer 181.

writings and rules of the Holy Fathers. St. Basil the Great offers to all who are illiterate, instead of the appointed prayers, the prayer of Jesus; and he does not offer it as a novelty but as a generally known exercise. This rule of St. Basil, with other traditions of the Eastern Church, passed from Greece to Russia, and many of the simple people with little education, and even those who were quite illiterate, found salvation and eternal life through the prayer of Jesus; many attained great spiritual proficiency.

St. John Chrysostom, in recommending the diligent and constant practice of the prayer of Jesus, especially for monks, speaks of it as of something widely known. "And we also have spiritual exorcisms," he says, "the name of our Lord Jesus Christ and the power of the cross. This exorcism not only drives the dragon out of his lair and casts him into the fire, but it even heals the wounds caused by him. If many used this exorcism and were not healed, this was due to their lack of faith and not to the ineffectualness of the exorcism. Although many constantly followed Christ and crowded round Him, yet they got no benefit. But the woman with an issue of blood, who did not touch His body but only the hem of His garment, had a long-standing flow of blood stopped. The name of Jesus Christ is terrible for demons, passions of the soul and diseases. Let us adorn and protect ourselves with it. Through it too Paul (the Apostle) became great, although he was of one nature with us."[1]

An Angel of God taught St. Pachomius the Great a rule of prayer for the vast community of monks dependent on him. The monks under the spiritual direction of St. Pachomius had to perform the rule every day. Only those

---

[1] On the Epistle to the Romans, Hom. 8.

who had attained perfection and the unceasing prayer connected with it were freed from the obligation to perform the
rule. The rule taught by the Angel consisted of the
Trisagion, the Lord's Prayer, Psalm 50, the Symbol of
Faith (Creed), and 100 Jesus Prayers. In the rule the
prayer of Jesus is spoken of like the Lord's prayer, that is,
as prayers generally known and in general use.

St. Barsanouphius the Great says that the principal occupation of the monks of Skete in Egypt was prayer. This is
also evident from the life of St. Pamba, monk and abba of
the Nitrian Mountain not far from Skete where, as in Skete,
the monks spent their life in silence. Of the saints of God
mentioned in this article who practised or wrote about the
prayer of Jesus, St. Ignatius the God-bearer lived in Antioch
and died in Rome; the holy martyr Kallistratus was a native
and inhabitant of Carthage; St. Pachomius the Great lived
in Upper Egypt; the monks of Skete and Nitria, like St.
Isaiah, lived in Lower Egypt; St. John Chrysostom lived in
Antioch and Constantinople; St. Basil the Great lived in
the eastern half of Asia Minor, in Cappadocia; St.
Barsanouphius the Great lived in the vicinity of Jerusalem;
St. John of the Ladder lived on Mount Sinai, and for some
time in Lower Egypt, near Alexandria. It is therefore
evident that prayer in the name of the Lord Jesus was universal,
in general use throughout the Catholic Church.

Besides the Fathers already mentioned, the following
also wrote about the prayer of Jesus: St. Hesychius, a priest
of Jerusalem, a disciple of St. Gregory the Theologian, a
writer of the fifth century, who already complains of the
neglect of the practice of the Prayer of Jesus and vigilance
by the monks of that time; St. Philotheus the Sinaite, St.
Symeon the New Theologian, St. Gregory the Sinaite, St.

Theolyptus of Philadelphia, St. Gregory Palamas, SS. Kallistus and Ignatius, and many others. Their writings are mostly to be found in that extensive collection of ascetic authors, the *Philokalia*. Russian Fathers who have written on the subject are St. Nile Sorsky, the holy monk Dorotheus, Archimandrite Païssy Velitchkovsky, the monk of the great habit Vasily Polyanomeroolsky, and Hieromonk Seraphim of Sarov.

All the writings of the Fathers we have named deserve deep study on account of the abundance of grace and spiritual understanding with which they are suffused and which they exhale. But the works of the Russian Fathers, on account of their special clarity and simplicity of expression and on account of their greater nearness to us in point of time, are more accessible to us than the writings of the Greek lights. In particular, the writings of the Elder Vasily can and should be recognised as the first book to which anyone who desires to practise the prayer of Jesus successfully in our time should certainly turn. And that is its purpose. The Elder called his writings preambles, introductions, or the sort of reading that prepares the way for the study of the Greek Fathers. An excellent book is that of St. Nile Sorsky. It should also be read before reading the Greek writers. It constantly refers to them and explains them, and so prepares the way for reading and understanding aright those deep-thinking, holy authors who are often rhetorical, philosophical and poetic.

Generally speaking, all the works of the Holy Fathers on the monastic life, and particularly on the prayer of Jesus, constitute for us monks of the last times a priceless treasure. In the times of St. Nile Sorsky, three[1] centuries before us,

---

[1] Now nearly four centuries ago. Brianchaninov wrote about 1860.

living vessels of divine grace were extremely rare, "had diminished exceedingly," according to his expression. Now they are so rare that it will scarcely be an exaggeration to say that they no longer exist. It is considered a very special mercy of God if anyone, exhausted in soul and body in the monastic life, towards the end of this life unexpectedly finds in some lonely place a vessel chosen by the impartial God, despised in the eyes of men, extolled and exalted by God. Thus Zosimus found in the uninhabited Transjordan desert, beyond all expectation, the great Mary of Egypt.[1] In view of the great scarcity of Spirit-bearing guides, the books of the Fathers constitute the only source to which a soul exhausted by hunger and thirst can turn to obtain the knowledge essentially necessary for the spiritual struggle. These books are the most precious heritage left by the Holy Fathers to us paupers, their spiritual descendants. These books are the crumbs which have fallen to us and constitute our share, crumbs from the spiritual table of the Fathers who were rich in gifts of the Spirit. It is remarkable that the time of writing of a great number of the books on mental prayer coincides with the time of the special decline of mental prayer in the monasteries. When St. Gregory the Sinaite, who lived in the 14th century, arrived on Mount Athos, he found there among the thousands of monks only three who had some understanding of mental prayer. Most of the writings on the prayer of Jesus belong to the 14th and 15th centuries.

"Moved by secret divine inspiration," writes Païssy Velitchkovsky, "many Fathers expounded in books the holy teaching, filled with the wisdom of the Holy Spirit, on this divine mental prayer, based on the Divine Scriptures of

---

[1] Lives of Saints, April 1st.

the Old and New Covenants. This was arranged by the special providence of God so that the divine activity should not pass into final oblivion. Many of these books, by God's permission, for our sins, were destroyed by the Moslems who conquered the Greek Empire; but by divine economy some have been preserved till our time."[1]

The most sublime mental activity is extraordinarily simple. It needs for its acceptance childlike simplicity and faith. But we have become so complicated that it is just this simplicity which is inaccessible, incomprehensible to us. We want to be clever, we want to revive our own *ego*, we cannot bear self-renunciation or self-denial, we have no desire to live and act by faith. It is for this reason that we need a guide to lead us out of our complexity, out of our cuteness, out of our cunning, out of our vanity and self-confidence, into the breadth and simplicity of faith. That is why it frequently happens that in the field of mental activity the child attains phenomenal success, while the learned man loses his way and falls into the dark pit of delusion.

"In ancient times," writes Païssy Velitchkovsky, "the most holy work of mental prayer shone in many places where the Holy Fathers lived, and there were then many guides for this spiritual labour. That is why when the Holy Fathers of those times wrote about it, they explained only the unspeakable spiritual profit which is derived from it. There was no need, I suppose, to write about that part of the work which belongs to beginners. They wrote to some extent even about that, which is very clear for those who have experimental knowledge of the subject; but for those who have not, it remains veiled. When some of the Fathers

---

[1] "Chapters on Mental Prayer," Ch. 1 (Optina edition, 1847).

saw that true and undeluded guides of this work had begun
to be very scarce, then moved by the Spirit of God, in order
that the true teaching on the elementary stages of this mental prayer should not be lost, they expounded in writing
the actual beginning, ways and exercises—how beginners
must train themselves to enter with the mind into the land
of the heart and there truly and without delusion perform
prayer with the mind."[1]

We have seen that the holy Prophet David invites all the
people of God without exception to prayer in the name of
the Lord. Saint Basil the Great, Archbishop of Caesarea
in Cappadocia, ruled that, for the illiterate and those who
do not know Sacred Scripture by heart, all the written
prayers should be replaced by the prayer of Jesus, and this
was accepted as a rule by the whole Eastern Church. Saint
Symeon, Archbishop of Salonika, orders and advises bishops,
priests, monks and lay people at all times and at every hour
to offer this sacred prayer and to make it, as it were, the
breath of their life. In the service of monastic profession,
when the newly-professed monk (or nun) is given the rosary,
the officiant says: "Receive, brother, the sword of the Spirit,
which is the word of God. Carry it on your lips, in your
mind and in your heart, and say unceasingly: Lord Jesus
Christ, Son of God, have mercy on me."

But St. Nile Sorsky teaches that "the remembrance of
God, that is, mental prayer is above all activities, (that it
is) the queen of virtues like the love of God. He who
shamelessly and audaciously wants to mount to God and
converse with Him directly, who strives to acquire Him
within himself, will be easily killed by demons if it is
allowed, as one who has audaciously and proudly sought

---

[1] "Chapters on Mental Prayer," Ch. 4 (Optina Edition, 1847).

THE PRAYER OF JESUS

to attain to what is above his merit and spirituality."[1]
This means that all Christians can and should practise the
prayer of Jesus for the purpose of repenting and calling
upon the Lord for help, with faith and the fear of God,
with the greatest attention to the thought and words of the
prayer, and with contrition of spirit. In this way not only
monks living in monasteries and engaged in obediences but
laypeople as well can and should practise the prayer of
Jesus. Such attentive prayer can be called both mental
and cordial as performed frequently with the mind alone
and in those who pray diligently always with the participation of the heart which expresses itself in a sense of sorrow
and tears of compunction. St. Nile Sorsky, basing himself on the teaching of all the Holy Fathers, forbids people
to strive prematurely for the union of the mind with the
heart, for the leading down of the mind into the heart, for
exterior and interior silence, for the feeling of devotion or
sweetness, and other high states of prayer; these are revealed when God accepts the prayer of penitence and the
enemies retreat from the soul. Said the Psalmist: *Depart
from me, all you workers of iniquity, for the Lord has heard
the voice of my weeping. The Lord has heard my petition,
the Lord has received my prayer* (Ps. 6: 9). Consolation,
comfort, joy and other spiritual gifts are consequences of
reconciliation. To seek them before reconciliation is an
undertaking fraught with indiscretion.

---

[1] Cp. "When a soul receives Me only as a friend, I allow her to
become sick, that she may call upon Me as a Physician."

PREPARATION FOR THE ART OF ARTS.

In order to acquire the deep prayer of the heart considerable preparation is necessary. This should consist in a thorough study of the monastic life by experience, and in training oneself for action according to the commandments of the Gospel, since holy prayer is based on a state of soul produced by action according to the commandments. It depends on that state and cannot exist in the soul when the soul is not in that state. Finally the preparation should consist in a thorough study of the New Testament and the writings of the Fathers on prayer. The last preparation is all the more indispensable since, owing to the lack of Spirit-bearing directors, our sole guide must be the writings of the Fathers and prayerful weeping before God. Very desirable is the prayer of the heart. Very desirable is the silence of the heart. Very desirable is it to remain perpetually enclosed in one's cell and to live in the most isolated desert, as these conditions are particularly favorable for the prayer of the heart and the silence of the heart. "But these very blessings and magnificent works," says St. Nile Sorsky, "must be practised with discretion and judgment, at the right time, when we have attained the due measure of progress, as Basil the Great says. Every work must be preceded by judgment. Without discretion even a good work is turned into an evil one by being untimely or excessive. But when the time and measure of the good work are determined with discretion, then a wonderful gain ensues. And Climacus,[1] borrowing the words from Scripture, says: *There is a time for everything under heaven* (Eccles. 3: 1), and among all things, he says, in our holy life as well there

---

[1] St. John of the Ladder.

is a time for every occupation. And, continuing, he says: There is a time for silence, and a time for unriotous talk; there is a time for unceasing prayer, and a time for honest service. Let us not be deluded by proud zeal and seek before the time what comes at a fixed time. Otherwise even in due time we shall receive nothing. There is a time to sow labours, and a time to reap the harvest of ineffable grace."[1] In particular St. Nile forbids an injudicious striving for solitude. Such striving nearly always makes its appearance in persons who understand neither themselves nor monasticism. It is because of this that the most serious self-deception and stumblings occur in solitude.

If it is forbidden for monks to strive prematurely for prayer offered by the mind in the temple of the heart, still more is it forbidden for laypeople. St. Andrew the Fool and a few others—extremely few laypeople—had the most profound prayer of the heart. This is an exception and the greatest rarity which cannot possibly serve as a rule for all. To class oneself among those exceptional personalities is nothing but self-deception due to conceit—hidden delusion prior to obvious delusions. Païssy Velitchkovsky in a letter to the Elder Theodosius says: "The books of the Fathers, especially those of them which teach true obedience, vigilance of mind and silence, attention and mental prayer (that is, prayer performed by the mind in the heart), are intended only for the monastic order and not for all Orthodox Christians in general. The God-bearing Fathers, in expounding the teaching on this prayer, affirm that its beginning and its unshakable foundation is true obedience, from which is born true humility; and humility guards him who labours in prayer from all the delusions which dog the

---

[1] Vol. II, Word 11 (cp. Ladder : 26, 87).

self-directed. But it is quite impossible for laypeople to acquire true monastic obedience and perfect denial[1] of the will and reason in everything. So how can laypeople without obedience, by self-direction which is accompanied by delusion, force themselves to such an awful and terrifying work, that is to such prayer, without any kind of guidance? How will they be able to escape the diverse and varied illusions of the enemy most cunningly directed against this prayer and those who practise it? So terrible is this thing (that is, prayer—not simply mental prayer, which is prayer performed by the mind unartistically, but prayer that acts artistically with the mind in the heart) that even those who are truly obedient and who have not only renounced[2] but have completely mortified their own will and judgment before their fathers, true and most experienced guides to the work of this prayer, are in constant fear and trembling, fearing and trembling lest they shall suffer from some kind of delusion in this prayer, although God always protects them from it for their true humility which they have acquired by the grace of God by means of their true obedience. How much more will laypeople living without obedience be in danger of falling into some kind of delusion if they force themselves to this prayer merely from reading books of this kind. This happens to those who begin the labour of this prayer on their own.

"The Saints called this prayer the art of arts. Who then can learn it without an artist, that is, without an experienced guide? This prayer is the spiritual sword given us by God for slaying the enemy of our souls. This prayer shone like the sun only among monks, especially in the lands of Egypt,

---

[1] "Denial." Lit. "cutting off."

[2] "Renounced." Lit. "cut off."

likewise in the lands of Jerusalem, on Mount Sinai and Nitria, in many parts of Palestine, and in many other places, but not everywhere, as is evident from the life of St. Gregory the Sinaite. He went over the whole of the holy mountain (Athos), and having made a diligent search for practisers of this prayer, he did not find a single one who had the least conception of this prayer.[1] Hence it is clear that if in such a holy place St. Gregory did not find a single person practising the prayer, in many places the practice of this prayer was unknown among monks. But where it was practised, where it shone like the sun among monks, there the practice of this prayer was guarded as a great and unutterable secret, known only to God and its practisers. To laypeople the practice of this prayer was completely unknown. But now, since the publication of the books of the Fathers, not only monks know about it, but all Christians as well. That is why I fear and tremble lest, for the reason mentioned above (that is, through entering upon the work of this prayer on their own, without a guide), such independent and self-directed souls may expose themselves to delusion, from which may Christ our Saviour deliver all who wish to be saved by His grace."[2]

---

[1] St. Gregory Sinaite visited Mount Athos in the 14th century. At that time monasticism in Palestine and Egypt had been practically wiped out by the Moslems who overran the Middle East in the 7th century. In St. Gregory's time mental prayer was everywhere practically unknown.

[2] "Life and Writings of the Moldavian Elder Paissy Velitchkovsky." Optina Hermitage edition, 1847.

THE SAFE WAY FOR BEGINNERS.

We consider it our duty to elucidate here, as far as our poor understanding and poor experience will allow, the teaching of the Holy Fathers on the artistic cultivation of the prayer of Jesus. We shall explain clearly how the prayer is to be practised, and what form of the prayer is suitable for all beginners without exception, whether monks or laymen, and what form of it is proper for proficients who have been raised to proficiency by God's will and God's grace.

Undoubtedly among all the ways the first place must be given to the way proposed by St. John of the Ladder, since it is particularly easy, absolutely safe, necessary and even indispensable if prayer is to be effectual; and it is suitable for all Christians living piously and seeking salvation, both monks and laypeople. The great director of monks twice speaks about this method in his Ladder which leads from earth to heaven—in his word on Obedience and in his word on prayer. The very fact that he expounds his method in the exposition of his teaching on obedience for monks living in community shows clearly that this method is intended even for novices. This method is described again at length in his separate teaching on prayer, after the instruction for hesychasts.[1] Consequently it is repeated for proficient monks. This shows clearly that the method is very good also for hesychasts and proficient monks. We repeat: the greatest advantage of this method consists in the fact that, besides being thoroughly satisfactory, it is absolutely safe. In his chapter on prayer St. John of the Ladder says: "Try to restore, or more exactly, to enclose

---

[1] Or, "those living in silence."

your thought in the words of the prayer. If on account of its infancy, it wearies and wanders lead it in again. The mind is naturally unstable. But He Who orders all things can control it. If you acquire this practice and constantly restrain it, *He Who sets bounds to the sea* of your mind will say to it during your prayer: *Hitherto thou shalt come, and shalt go no further* (Job 38: 11). It is impossible to bind a spirit. But where the Creator of that spirit is present, there everything obeys Him."[1] "The beginning of prayer consists in banishing the thoughts that come to us, at their very appearance; the middle is when the mind stays solely in the words pronounced vocally or mentally."[2] In the chapter on Obedience, St. John says: "Constantly struggle with your thought, and whenever it is carried hither and thither, collect it together. God does not require from novices prayer completely free from distractions. Do not despond when your thought is distracted, but remain calm, and unceasingly restore your mind to itself."[3]

Here is taught a method of praying attentively, of praying both vocally and with the mind alone. In attentive prayer the heart cannot help taking part, as St. Mark has said: "The mind which prays without distraction constrains the heart." Thus, he who prays by the method proposed by St. John of the Ladder will pray with the lips and with the mind and with the heart. And when he becomes proficient in prayer, he will acquire mental prayer and the prayer of the heart, and he will attract divine grace to himself, as is evident from the words we have quoted of the great director of monks. What more can be desired?

---

[1] Ladder : 28 : 17.

[2] Ibid. 28 : 19.

[3] Ibid. 4 : 93.

Nothing. What delusion can there be in this way of praying? Only thought-wandering and distraction. But this
is a fault that is completely obvious, inevitable in beginners, but capable of immediate treatment through the
restoration of the thought to the words. Moreover, by the
mercy and help of God, with constant effort, distraction is
eventually eliminated

It may be asked, does such a great Father who lived at a
time when mental prayer flourished actually say nothing
about prayer performed by the mind in the heart? He
speaks about it, but in such a veiled manner that only those
who know by experience the work of prayer can understand
what he is talking about. The Saint acted in this way by
the guidance of the spirit of wisdom with which his whole
book is written. In explaining the truest and most satisfactory teaching on prayer which can lead the person who
practises it to a state of grace, Climacus spoke figuratively
about what is accomplished when the labour of prayer is
blessed with grace. "It is one thing," he said, "frequently
to look into the heart, and another to entrust the watch of
the heart to the mind, that prince and bishop that offers
spiritual sacrifices to Christ."[1] It is one thing to pray with
attention with the participation of the heart; it is another
thing to descend with the mind into the temple of the heart
and from there to offer mystical prayer filled with divine
grace and power. The second is a result of the first. The
attention of the mind during prayer draws the heart into
sympathy. With the strengthening of the attention, sympathy
of heart and mind is turned into union of heart and mind.
Finally when the attention makes the prayer its own, the

[1] Ladder: 28 : 51.

mind descends into the heart for the most profound and sacred service of prayer.

All this is accomplished under the guidance of the grace of God, at His pleasure and discretion. To strive for the second before acquiring the first is not only useless but can cause the greatest harm. To obviate this harm the mystery of prayer is veiled from curiosity and levity in a book intended for the use of monks in general. In those blessed times, when there were plenty of living vessels of grace, people could resort to their counsel in all cases needing special advice.

Among the monks of Raithu for whom St. John wrote his "Ladder," mental prayer flourished under the guidance of skilled spiritual direction. The holy author alludes to this, again in an allegorical and veiled manner, in his "Word to the Pastor" thus: "Above all, venerable father, we need spiritual power if we are to be able to take by the hand like children and deliver from the crowd of thoughts those whom we desire to lead into the Holy of Holies and to whom we hope to show Christ resting on their mystical and hidden table—especially as long as they are in the forecourt of that entrance, and when we see that the crowd is pressing and oppressing them with the object of preventing the entry they desire. But if the children are extremely weak and naked, we must lift them on to our shoulders and carry them on our shoulders until they pass through the door of the entrance. I know for certain that there is usually much crowding and pressing there. That is why someone said of this press: *This labour is before me until I enter the sanctuary of God* (Ps. 72: 17). But the labour lasts only till the entrance."[1]

---

[1] "Word to the Pastor," ch. 14.

"He who desires to see the Lord within himself endeavours to purify his heart by the unceasing remembrance of God. The spiritual land of a man pure in soul is within him. The sun which shines in it is the light of the Holy Trinity. The air which its inhabitant breathes is the All-holy Spirit. The life, joy and gladness of that country is Christ, the Light of the Light—the Father. That is the Jerusalem or Kingdom of God hidden *within us,* according to the word of the Lord.[1] Try to enter the cell within you, and you will see the heavenly cell. They are one and the same. By one entry you enter both. The ladder to the Heavenly Kingdom is within you. It is built mysteriously in your soul. Immerse yourself within yourself beyond the reach of sin, and you will find there steps by which you can mount to heaven."[2]

TEACHING OF ST. BARSANOUPHIUS, DOROTHEUS THE RUSSIAN, AND ST. SERAPHIM.

St. Barsanouphius, a monk who reached the highest degree of spiritual proficiency, also led his disciples into the sanctuary of grace-given prayer of the heart and to the levels of spirituality which are the fruit of it. Among his instructions is the following, given to a hermit under his direction: "May the one sinless God Who saves those who trust in Him, strengthen your love to serve Him in holiness and righteousness all the days of your life, in the temple and altar of the inner man where spiritual sacrifices are offered to God—gold, incense and myrrh—where the fatted calf is slain, where the precious blood of the immaculate Lamb is

---

[1] S. Isaac the Syrian, ch. 8.
[2] Ibid., ch. 2.

sprinkled, where the harmonious shouts of Holy Angels re-echo: *Then they will offer calves on Thy altar* (Ps. 50: 21). Then! When? When our Lord comes, that great High Priest Who offers and receives the bloodless sacrifice; when, in His name, the lame man sitting at the beautiful gates is granted to hear the joyful voice: *Rise and walk* (Acts 3: 6). Then the lame man enters the sanctuary, walking and leaping and praising God. Then the sleep of negligence and ignorance ceases; then the drowsiness of sloth and despondency is whisked from the eyelids; then the five wise virgins light their lamps and rejoice with the Bridegroom in the holy bedchamber, singing in harmony, silently: *Taste and see that the Lord is good. Blessed is the man who hopes in Him* (Ps. 38: 4). Then conflicts, pollutions and movements cease. Then is established the holy peace of the Holy Trinity, the treasure is sealed and remains secure. Pray that you may realize and attain it, and rejoice in Jesus Christ our Lord."[1]

The greatest reverence for contemplative prayer of the heart is inspired by the sublime descriptions of it in the writings of the Fathers. We need this reverence and real vision in order to renounce all premature, self-willed, proud, imprudent striving to enter the secret sanctuary. And reverence and wisdom teach us to wait with attentive prayer, the prayer of penitence, at the doors of the temple. Attention and contrition of spirit—that is the waiting-room[2] that is given as a haven to penitent sinners.

It is the forecourt of the sanctuary. There let us hide and shut ourselves from sin. Let all suffering from moral or spiritual lameness, all lepers, all the blind and withered,

---

[1] Answer 115.

[2] "Waiting-room." Lit. "cell."

in a word all who are sick with sin, come to that Bethesda and *wait for a movement of the water* (Jn. 5: 3)—the action of the mercy and grace of God. And the One Lord Himself, at a time known to Him, will grant healing and the entry into the sanctuary, solely according to His inscrutable will. *I know whom I have chosen,* says the Saviour (Jn. 13: 18). *You did not choose Me,* He says to His chosen, *but I chose you and appointed you that you should go and bear fruit; so that whatever you ask the Father in My name, He may give it to you* (Jn. 15: 16).

Extremely good is the method of practising the prayer of Jesus taught by Dorotheus, the Russian ascetic and spiritual writer. "He who prays with the lips," he says, "but neglects his soul and does not guard his heart, prays to the air and not to God; and he labours in vain, because God attends to the mind and fervour, and not to prolixity. One should pray with all one's fervour, with one's soul and mind and heart, with the fear of God, and with all one's strength. Mental prayer does not allow either distractions or foul thoughts to enter the inner sanctum. Do you wish to learn to pray with the mind and heart? I will teach you. A first you should make the prayer of Jesus with your voice, that is, with your lips, tongue and speech, aloud by yourself. When the lips, tongue and senses are satisfied with prayer pronounced vocally, then vocal prayer stops and it begins to be said in a whisper. After this one should contemplate with the mind, and always regard and attend diligently to the feeling in the throat. Then mental prayer of the heart constantly begins to rise automatically by the nod (of God)[1]— begins to be carried about and act at all times, during every kind of work, in every place."

---

[1] That is, by the action of divine grace.

The blessed elder, Hieromonk Seraphim of Sarov, orders the beginner, according to a previously existing general custom in Sarov Monastery, to make unceasingly the prayer: *Lord Jesus Christ, Son of God, have mercy on me, a sinner.* "During prayer," teaches the elder, "attend to yourself, that is, collect your mind and unite it with your soul. At first, for a day or two or more, make this prayer with the mind alone, slowly, attending to every word separately. When the Lord warms your heart with the warmth of His grace and unites you in one spirit,[1] then this prayer will flow within you unceasingly and will always be with you, delighting and nourishing you. And that is exactly what the words spoken by the Prophet Isaiah mean: *The dew which is with Thee is healing for them* (Is. 26: 19). But when you contain within you this food of the soul, that is, converse with the Lord, why go from cell to cell of the brethren, even though you are invited by someone? Truly I tell you, idle-talking is love of idleness. If you do not understand yourself, can you discuss anything or teach others? Be silent, constantly be silent. Remember always the presence of God and His name. Do not enter into conversation with anyone: but at the same time beware of judging those who talk and laugh. In that case be deaf and dumb. Whatever people say about you, let it all go past your ears. As a model for yourself you can take Stephen the New whose prayer was unceasing, conduct meek, mouth silent, heart humble, spirit contrite, body and soul pure, virginity spotless, poverty true and detachment eremetic; his obedience was unmurmuring, his activity

---

[1] Very few receive the union of the mind with the heart soon after starting the work of prayer. Usually many years pass before that takes place. We must prove the sincerity of our will by perseverance and patience (Brianchaninov).

patient, his labour fervent. When sitting at table, do not look to see and criticise how much anyone eats, but attend to yourself and feed your soul with prayer."[1]

Having given this instruction to a beginner leading an active life in monastic labours and having taught him an exercise of prayer suitable to an active person, the Elder forbids a premature and injudicious striving for the contemplative life and for the prayer corresponding to that life. "Everyone," he says, "who wishes to live a spiritual life must begin with the active life and afterwards pass to the contemplative, because without the active life it is impossible to come to the contemplative. The active life serves to purify us from sinful passions and leads us to a degree of active perfection, and in this way it opens for us the way to the contemplative life. Only those who have been purified from the passions and have had a thorough training in the active life can proceed to the contemplative life. This can be seen from the words of Sacred Scripture, *blessed are the pure in heart, for they shall see God* (Matt. 5: 8), and from the words of St. Gregory the Theologian: 'Only after their experience (in the active life) can the more perfect proceed to contemplation.' One should approach the contemplative life with fear and trembling, with contrition of heart and humility, with much searching of Holy Scripture, and under the direction of a skilled elder if such can be found, and not with presumption and self-confidence. An audacious and scornful man, according to the words of Gregory the Sinaite, having sought (a high spiritual state) for which he is not fit, conceitedly strives to attain it prematurely. And again: If anyone dreams by his own mind to attain a high state and has acquired a satanic

---

[1] Instruction 32.

and not a true desire, him the devil catches in his nets as
his servant."[1]

While thus warning against a proud striving for a high
state of prayer, the elder insists on the necessity for all
monks in general, including the most elementary novices, of
a recollected life and unceasing prayer. It has been
observed that for the most part that tendency which is
accepted on his entry into the monastery remains dominant
in a monk for the whole of his life. "Only those who have
interior prayer and watch over their souls receive the gifts
of grace," affirms St. Seraphim.[2] "Those who have truly
resolved to serve God must practise the remembrance of
God and unceasing prayer to the Lord Jesus Christ, saying
with the mind: *Lord Jesus Christ, Son of God, have mercy
on me, a sinner.* By this practice, while guarding oneself
from distraction and while maintaining peace of conscience,
one can draw near to God and be united with Him. Other
than by unceasing prayer, according to the words of St.
Isaac the Syrian, it is impossible to draw near to God."[3]

To avoid distraction and remain recollected St. Seraphim
advises monks and novices who wish to practise the prayer
of Jesus to stand in church during the services with closed
eyes, and to open them only when oppressed by sleep and
drowsiness. Then he advises them to direct their gaze
towards the holy ikons, which also prevents distraction and
stimulates prayer.[3]

A beginner can learn the prayer of Jesus with special
ease during the long monastic services. When present at
them, what is the use of fruitlessly and harmfully allowing

---

[1] Instruction 29.
[2] Instruction 4.
[3] Instruction 11.

one's thoughts to wander everywhere? But this is impossible to avoid unless the mind is fixed on something. Busy yourself with the prayer of Jesus. It will prevent the mind from wandering. You will become far more recollected, more deeply concentrated. You will attend much better to the church reading and singing. And at the same time in an imperceptible manner you will gradually train yourself in mental prayer.

St. Seraphim orders one who desires to live a recollected life not to attend to irrelevant rumours which fill the head with vain and idle thoughts and memories, and not to pay attention to the affairs of others, not to judge them, and not even to think or speak about them. He orders such a person to avoid conversations, to behave like a pilgrim or stranger, to bow in silence to fathers and brothers whom one happens to meet and to guard oneself from looking attentively at them,[1] because such looking cannot fail to produce in the soul some kind of impression which will cause distraction by drawing away the attention and diverting it from prayer. Generally speaking, one living a recollected life should not stare[2] at anything, and should not listen to anything with special diligence, but should see as if without seeing and hear as if in passing, so that the memory and power of attention may be always free, immune to the impressions of the world, apt and ready to receive the divine impressions.

---

[1] Instruction 6.
[2] "Stare." Lit. "look fixedly."

THE METHOD OF ST. JOHN OF THE LADDER

It is evident that the methods proposed by the monk Dorotheus and the elder Seraphim are identical with the method proposed by St. John of the Ladder. But St. John has expounded his method with special clarity and precision. This Father is among the most ancient and greatest of the guides of monasticism, and is recognised as such by the Universal Church. Later holy writers refer to him as a most reliable teacher, as a living vessel of the Holy Spirit. On these grounds we offer his method with complete confidence to beloved fathers and brothers, not only those living in monasteries, but also those living in the midst of the world who have an honest desire to pray sincerely, successfully and in a way pleasing to God—for general use. This method is indispensable. To dispense with the method would be to dispense with attention. But without attention prayer is not prayer. It is dead! It is useless, soul-harming babbling, offensive to God. He who prays attentively cannot fail to pray more or less by this method. If the attention grows and increases during prayer, the method of prayer offered by the divine John will certainly make its appearance. "*Ask* with tears," he says, "*seek* with obedience, *knock* with patience. In this way, *he who asks receives, he who seeks finds, and to him who knocks it will be opened* (Matt. 7: 8)."[1]

Experience will soon show that in using this method, especially at first, the words should be pronounced with extreme unhurriedness so that the mind may have time to enter the words as into forms. This cannot be done when the reading is hurried. St. John's method is very con-

---

[1] Ladder 28: 56.

venient both when practising the prayer of Jesus and when
reading the ordinary prayers in one's cell, and even when
reading the Scriptures and patristic books.   One must train
oneself to it as if one were reading by syllables—with the
same unhurriedness.   He who has become proficient in this
method has acquired oral, mental and cordial prayer suitable for anyone living an active life.   The most holy
Kallistos, Patriarch of Constantinople, delivers the following judgment on prayer: "Unceasing prayer consists in an
unceasing invocation of the name of God.   Whether talking, sitting, walking, making something, eating or occupied
in some other way, one should at all times and in every
place call upon the name of God, according to the command of Scripture: *Pray without ceasing* (1 Thess. 5: 17).
In this way the enemy's attempts upon our life are foiled.
We must pray with the heart; we must also pray with the
mouth, when we are alone.   But if we are in the market, or
in the company of others, we should not pray with the lips,
but only with the mind.   We must keep watch over our
sight and always look down to guard ourselves from distraction and the enemy's snares.   Prayer has reached perfection when it is offered to God without the mind's wandering into distraction, when all a person's thoughts and
feelings are gathered into one prayer.   Prayer and psalmody
should be performed not only with the mind but with the
mouth too, as the Prophet David says: *O Lord, open my
lips, and my mouth shall declare Thy praise* (Ps. 50: 17).   And
the Apostle, showing that the mouth is required as well,
said: *Let us offer to God a sacrifice of praise, that is, the fruit
of lips that confess His name* (Heb. 13: 15)."

To a monk who asked him how to pray St. Barsanouphius
the Great replied: "We should exercise ourselves in

psalmody to some extent, and pray vocally to some extent. We also need time to examine and observe our thoughts. He who at dinner has many different foods eats much and with pleasure, whereas he who uses every day the same food not only eats it without pleasure but sometimes perhaps even feels repelled by it. So it is in our state. In psalmody and prayer do not bind yourself, but do as much as the Lord gives you. Do not abandon reading and interior prayer either. Some of one and some of the other—and so you will spend the day pleasing God. Our perfect fathers did not have a fixed rule, but during the course of the whole day they carried out their rule. They exercised themselves in psalmody to some extent, to some extent prayed orally, to some extent examined their thoughts, and they even gave a little time and thought to food. But they did all this with the fear of God."[1]

That is how a holy Father who had become very proficient in prayer instructed a brother. Experience will teach everyone who practises prayer that the saying aloud of a few prayers of Jesus and all prayers in general is a great help in preventing the mind from being robbed by distraction. In the event of a violent attack of the enemy, when a weakening of the will and darkening of the mind is felt, vocal prayer is indispensable. Attentive vocal prayer is at the same time both mental and cordial.

By our poor word we are not preventing or deterring our beloved fathers and brothers from eminent success in prayer. On the contrary, we desire it with all our heart. May all monks be like Angels and Archangels who have no rest day or night from the divine love which stimulates them and are therefore incessantly and insatiably satisfied

---

[1] Answer 177.

with glorifying God. For the very reason that the price-less wealth of the prayer of the heart that is a gift of grace may be received in its time we forbid and warn our readers against striving for it prematurely, from proudly consider-ing yourself worthy and fit to receive it, and thereby depriv-ing yourself of it. This striving is forbidden because the discovery in oneself of the prayer of grace by one's own efforts is impossible. This striving which crashes furiously against the gates of the mystical temple of God is forbidden in order that it may not prevent the mercy of God from eventually having mercy on us, and regarding the unworthy as worthy, and giving the gift to those who were not expect-ing the gift, having doomed themselves to eternal torments in the prisons of hell.

The gift is given to those who humble and abase them-selves before the greatness of the gift. The gift is given to those who renounce their own will and surrender them-selves to the will of God. The gift is given to those who subdue and mortify their flesh and blood, who subdue and mortify the mind of the flesh by the commandments of the Gospel. Life dawns and rises according to the degree of our mortification. It comes unexpectedly, entirely at its own good pleasure, and then it completes and perfects the mortification begun voluntarily. Careless, especially self-willed, proud and self-directed seekers of a high state of prayer are always sealed with the seal of rejection, with the precision of spiritual law (Matt. 22: 12-14). The removal of that seal is very difficult, mostly impossible. Why? Because pride and self-confidence which lead to self-deception, to fellowship with demons and enslavement to them, do not allow us to see the wrongness and peril of our positions, do not allow us to see our woeful fellowship with the demons, nor our disastrous, fatal enslavement to them. "Clothe yourself first with leaves, and then when God commands bring the fruits," said the Fathers.[1] First acquire attentive prayer. To one purified and prepared by attentive prayer, trained and qualified by the commandments of the Gospel and grounded on them, God—the all-merciful God—will give in His time the prayer of Grace.

God is the teacher of prayer; true prayer is the gift of God.[2] To him who prays constantly with contrition of spirit, with the fear of God and with attention, God Himself gives gradual progress in prayer. From humble and attentive prayer, spiritual action and spiritual warmth make their appearance and quicken the heart. The quickened heart draws the mind to itself and becomes a temple of grace-given prayer and a treasury of the spiritual gifts which are procured by such prayer as a matter of course.

"Labour away," say great ascetics and teachers of prayer, "with pain of heart to obtain warmth and prayer, and God will grant you to have them always. Forgetfulness expels them, and it is born of sloth and carelessness."[3] If you want to be delivered from forgetfulness and captivity, you will not be able to attain it otherwise than by acquiring within you the spiritual fire; only from the warmth of the fire of the Spirit forgetfulness and captivity vanish. This fire is obtained by desire for God. Brother! Unless your heart seeks the Lord day and night with pain, you will not be able to succeed. But if you abandon everything else and occupy yourself with this, you will attain it, as Scripture says: *Be still and realise* (Ps. 45: 11). Brother! Implore

---

[1] St. Barsanouphius the Great and John the Prophet: Answer 325.

[2] Ladder: 28: 64.

[3] St. Barsanouphius and John: Answers 264, 274 and 273.

the goodness of Him Who *desires all men to be saved and to come to the knowledge of the truth* (1 Tim. 2: 4) to give you spiritual vigilance which kindles the spiritual fire. The Lord of heaven and earth came to earth to pour that fire upon it (Lk. 12: 49). According to my power I shall pray with you that God Who gives grace to all who ask with fervour and toil may grant you that vigilance. When it comes it will guide you to the truth. It enlightens the eyes, directs the mind, banishes the sleep of languor and negligence, restores lustre to the weapon covered with rust in the earth of sloth, restores radiance to clothes defiled by captivity to barbarians, inspires a desire to be satisfied with the great sacrifice offered by our great High Priest. This sacrifice of which it was revealed to the Prophet that it cleanses sins and takes away iniquities (Is. 6: 7), forgives those who weep, and gives grace to the humble (Prov. 3: 34), manifests itself in the worthy, and by it they inherit eternal life, in the name of the Father, the Son and the Holy Spirit.

"Spiritual vigilance or sobriety is a spiritual art which completely delivers a man, with the help of God, from sinful actions and passionate thoughts and words when fervently practised for a considerable time. It is silence of heart; it is guarding of the mind; it is attention to oneself without any other thought which always, incessantly and unceasingly calls upon Jesus Christ, the Son of God and God, which breathes by Him, with Him courageously takes up arms against the enemies, and which confesses Him." This is the definition of spiritual vigilance that St. Hesychius of Jerusalem gives.[1] The rest of the Fathers agree with him.

---

[1] On Sobriety or Vigilance : Chs. 1, 3 and 5 (Philokalia).

"When the fire descends into the heart," says St. John of the Ladder, "it revives prayer. And when prayer has risen and ascended to heaven, then the descent of the fire takes place into the cenacle of the soul."[1] It is evident that the saint is speaking from his own blessed experience. Something similar happened in the case of St. Maximus Kapsokalivitis. "From my youth," he told St. Gregory the Sinaite, "I had great faith in my Lady, the Mother of God, and besought her with tears to grant me the grace of mental prayer. Once I came to her temple as usual and fervently prayed to her for this. I went up to her ikon and reverently kissed her image. Suddenly I felt as if there fell into my breast and heart a warmth which did not burn, but bedewed and delighted me, and stirred my soul to compunction. From that moment my *heart* began to say the prayer within itself, and my *mind* began to delight in the remembrance of my Jesus and the Mother of God and to have Him, the Lord Jesus, constantly within itself. Since then the prayer has never ceased in my *heart*."[2]

The prayer of grace appeared suddenly, unexpectedly, as a gift from God. The Saint's soul had been prepared to received the gift of prayer by fervent, attentive, humble, constant prayer. The prayer of grace did not stay in the Saint without its usual concomitants, quite unknown and uncongenial to the carnal and natural state.

An abundant manifestation of spiritual fire in the heart, the fire of divine love, is described by George, the recluse of Zadonsk, from his own experience. But before that, he was sent the divine gift of penitence which purified his hear to receive love (the gift which acts like fire and con-

[1] Ladder : 28 : 45.
[2] Philokalia.

sumes all that defiles the courts of the Holy and Mighty Lord), and even took all the strength from his body. "The holy and heavenly fire," says St. John of the Ladder, "scorches some on account of their defective purity; but others it enlightens as having attained perfection. The same fire is called a consuming fire and an illuminating light. For this reason some leave their prayer as if it were a hotly heated bath-house, feeling a certain relief from defilement and earthliness; while others go out shining with light and arrayed in a double garment of joy and humility. But those who after prayer feel neither of these two effects are still praying bodily, and not spiritually."[1] Prayer inspired by divine grace is here called spiritual prayer, while prayer performed by one's own efforts without the obvious assistance of grace is called bodily prayer. The latter kind of prayer is indispensable, as St. John of the Ladder says, in order that grace-given prayer may be granted in its time. But how does the prayer of grace intimate its coming? It intimates its coming by supernatural weeping—and the man enters the gates of God's sanctuary (his heart) with unspeakable thankfulness.

HIGHER LEVELS OF PRAYER

Before coming to a description of the method offered by the holy Fathers almost exclusively to those living in silence, we consider it necessary to prepare the reader somewhat. The writings of the Fathers may be compared to a chemist's shop (drug-store) in which are quantities of the

---

[1] Ladder : 28: 51.

most healing remedies. But a sick man unacquainted with medical science and without a doctor for a guide will find it very difficult to select a medicine suitable to his illness. But if out of self-confidence and thoughtlessness, without properly consulting, in the absence of a doctor, medical books, the sick man hurriedly decides on the choice of a medicine himself, that choice can be most unfortunate. A medicine in itself curative can prove not only useless but even very harmful. We are in a position similar to that of the sick man owing to the absence of Spirit-bearing guides in regard to the writings of the holy Fathers on the mystical action of the prayer of the heart and its consequences. The teaching on prayer in the books of the Fathers that have come down to us is expounded with satisfying fulness and clarity. But being placed in our ignorance before these books in which are described in the greatest variety the activities and states of beginners, intermediates and proficients, we find it extremely difficult to choose states and activities suitable for us. Unspeakably happy is he who feels and reliases this difficulty. Through not realising it, after a superficial reading of the holy Fathers and having become superficially acquainted with the activities proposed by them, many have taken upon themselves an activity unsuited to them, and have done themselves harm.

St. Gregory the Sinaite,[1] in his article written for the extremely advanced hesychast Longinus, says: "The work of silence is one thing, and life in community is another. Everyone who continues in the life to which he is called will be saved. And therefore I am afraid to write on account of the weak, knowing that you live among them.

---

[1] See art. "How to Sing" in Philokalia.

For whoever adopts an excessively strenuous labour of prayer from hearsay or study labours in vain[1] through having no director." The holy Fathers remind us that many who undertake the work of prayer wrongly, by methods for which they were unready or unfit, fell into self-delusion and mental derangement.

The greatest harm comes not only from reading the books of the Fathers with insufficient understanding but even from associating with the greatest of God's saints and from hearing their holy teaching. That is what happened to the Syrian monk Malpat. He was a disciple of St. Julian. In the company of his Elder (St. Julian), Malpat visited St. Antony the Great and heard from him the most sublime teaching on the monastic life: on self-mortification, on mental prayer, on purity of soul, on vision. Without properly understanding his teaching, burning with material heat, Malpat laid upon himself the severest labour and began to live as a strict recluse, in the hope of attaining that high spiritual state of which he had heard from Antony the Great, and which he had seen and touched in Antony the Great. The result of his effort was the most fearful self-deception. Corresponding to his violent effort there was formed a violent delusion, while the conceit which seized the unfortunate man's soul rendered him incapable of repentance and so of healing. Malpat became the inventor and head of the heresy of the Euchites.[2] O sad event! O most sad spectacle! A disciple of a great Saint, after hearing the teaching of the greatest of Saints, through wrongly putting their teaching into practice, perished. He perished in those times when, on account of the hosts of

---

[1] "Labours in vain." Brianchaninov has "perishes."

[2] St. Isaac the Syrian : Ch. 55.

saints able to direct and heal, very few souls were lost through delusion.

This is said as a warning to us. When countless lights existed, the way of interior monasticism—mystical prayer in solitude and the silence of the mind in the heart—was recognized as a way beset with dangers. How much more perilous is this way now that the dark night has come! Dense clouds and fog hide the heavenly lights. One must travel extremely slowly, groping one's way. The study of the patristic books provided by Divine Providence as the moral guidance for contemporary monasticism is no trifling enterprise. In order to succeed in it, self-renunciation is necessary; the abandonment of worldly cares is necessary —not to mention diversions, amusements and pleasures; it is necessary to live according to the commandments of the Gospel; necessary too is purity of mind and heart by which alone the spiritual, holy and mystical teaching of the Spirit can be discerned and understood according to the degree of one's purification. Let him who has learnt that at the present time the treasure of salvation and Christian perfection is hidden in the words uttered by the Holy Spirit or under His influence, that is, in Sacred Scripture and the writings of the Holy Fathers, rejoice spiritually that he has obtained really useful knowledge, let him hide completely from the world in a pious life, *let him go and sell all that he has and buy that field* (Matt. 13: 44), in which is hidden salvation and perfection.

To make a thorough study of Scripture, with corresponding practice, considerable time is necessary. After a thorough study of Scripture, with the greatest caution, constantly asking God's help by prayer and weeping, in poverty of spirit, one may even attempt those activities which lead to perfection. A certain holy monk said of himself that he studied the writings of the Fathers for twenty years while leading the ordinary life of a monk in community. At the end of that time he decided to become practically acquainted with the profound monastic activity, a theoretical knowledge of which he had acquired by reading, and probably, as was possible at that time, from conversations with proficient Fathers. The progress of a monk by the guidance of reading is incomparably slower than by the guidance of a Spirit-bearing director.

What is written by every holy writer is written from his spiritual level (attainment) and from his practice (experience), in conformity with his level and practice. We must pay special attention to this point. Let us not be carried away and enraptured by a book written as if with fire that tells of high states and activities for which we are unfit. The reading of such a book, by firing the imagination, can harm us by communicating a knowledge of and desire for labours that are untimely and impossible for us. Let us apply ourselves to the book of a Father nearer to our state in the matter of attainment. With this view of patristic books one may offer as the first reading of a monk who desires to become acquainted with the work of interior prayer the instructions of St. Seraphim of Sarov, and the works of Païssy Velitchkovsky and his friend, the monk of the great habit Basil. The holiness of these persons and the soundness of their teaching is undoubted. After studying these writings, one can turn to the book of St. Nile Sorsky. This book is small in format, but its spiritual scope is extraordinarily comprehensive. It would be difficult to find a question on mental activity which is not solved in it. Everything is explained with quite extraordinary simplicity and clarity in a most satisfying manner. The method of practising the prayer of Jesus is similarly explained. But both the method and the whole book are intended for monks capable of living in silence.[1]

TEACHING OF ST. NILE SORSKY.

St. Nile prescribes *silence of the mind*, and not only does not allow one to think of anything vain or sinful, but what is apparently profitable, and even what is spiritual, is also banned. Instead of all thought he orders one to gaze unceasingly into the depth of one's heart and say, *Lord Jesus Christ, Son of God, have mercy on me, a sinner.* One may pray standing, sitting or lying. Those who are strong in health and physique pray standing and sitting. The weak can pray even lying, because in this prayer it is not the effort of the body that is paramount, but the effort of the spirit. The body should be given a position that allows the spirit full freedom to act properly. It must be borne in mind that we are speaking here of the prayer of monks who by sufficient bodily labour have reduced their bodily impulses to due order and on account of their proficiency have passed from bodily to spiritual labour.

St. Nile orders one to enclose the mind in the heart and to check the breathing as far as possible so as not to inhale frequently. That means that one must breathe very slowly. In general all stirrings of the flesh and blood must be restrained, and both body and soul must be held in a

---

[1] "Silence" here has a technical signification, and may be rendered "hesychasm."

restful position, in a state of calm, reverence and the fear of God. Without this the spiritual action cannot appear in us. It makes its appearance when all the stirrings of the blood and impulses of the flesh abate. Experience will soon teach that the checking of the breathing (that is, an infrequent and gentle inhalation of breath) greatly assists the recollection of the mind from wandering.

"There are many virtuous actions," says St. Nile, "but they are all particular. But the prayer of the heart is the source of all blessings. It waters the soul like gardens. This activity which consists in the watching of the mind in the heart, outside all thoughts, is extremely difficult for those who have not been trained to it. It is difficult not only for beginners, but even for those who have laboured long but who have not yet received or retained within the heart the sweetness of prayer from the action of grace. It is well-known from experience that for the weak this work seems very wearisome and hard. But when one obtains grace, then he prays without difficulty and with love, being comforted by grace. When *the effect*[1] of prayer comes, then it draws the mind to itself, fills it with joy and delivers it from distraction."[2]

In order to learn the method proposed by St. Nile Sorsky, it is very good to combine it with the method of St. John of the Ladder, and to pray very unhurriedly. In expounding his method, St. Nile refers to many Fathers of the Church, but especially to St. Gregory the Sinaite.

The writings of St. Gregory the Sinaite, though having full spiritual merit, are nevertheless not so accessible and clear as those of St. Nile Sorsky. The reason for this is the manner of exposition, and the fact that the ideas of

---

[1] The effect: or, the action. [2] Word 2.

that time on various subjects are more remote for us, especially the spiritual proficiency of the person who wrote the book and of the person for whom the book was written. The method of prayer proposed by the Sinaite is almost the same as that proposed by Nile who borrowed his doctrine of prayer from reading and studying the Sinaite's book, and from oral conversations with disciples of the Sinaite on his visi: to the East.

ST. GREGORY THE SINAITE.

"*In the morning*," says St. Gregory quoting the Wisdom of Solomon, "*sow thy seed*, that is, prayer, *and in the evening let not thy hand cease*, lest the constancy of prayer, broken by intervals, should lose that hour in which it might be heard; *for thou knowest not which may spring up* (Eccles. 11: 6). In the morning sit on a stool the height of a span, and lead your mind down from your head into your heart, and hold it there; bending forward painfully and having much pain in the chest, neck and shoulders, unceasingly cry with the mind or soul: *Lord Jesus Christ, have mercy on me.* And restrain your breathing somewhat, so as not to breathe carelessly."[1]

Regarding the teaching that the breathing should be checked, the Sinaite quotes Saints Isaiah the Solitary, John of the Ladder, and Symeon the New Theologian.

"If we wish unerringly to find the truth and know it," says the Sinaite, "let us endeavour to have solely the action of the heart. It must be completely imageless and we must on no account give freedom to the imagination or allow

---

[1] On Silence in 15 chapters : ch. 2 and 3.

the fancy to form an image of any saint or light; because usually delusions, especially at the beginning of the work, deceive the minds of the inexperienced with false phantasies of this kind. Let us strive to have in an active heart only *the action* of prayer which warms and gladdens the mind, and inflames the soul to unutterable love for God and man. Then observable humility and contrition makes its appearance from the prayer, because prayer in beginners is the ever-moving mental *action* of the Holy Spirit. This action at the beginning is like a fire that flares up in the heart, but at the end it is like a fragrant light."[1]

By beginners is meant here beginners in silence (hesychasm). In fact, the whole of St. Gregory the Sinaite's book is intended for the instruction of hesychasts. Again the holy Sinaite says: "Some teach that the prayer should be said vocally, others—with the mind alone. But I recommend both ways. For sometimes the mind gets exhausted in saying the prayer from tedium, and sometimes the mouth wearies of doing so. Therefore we should pray with both, with the mouth and with the mind. Yet we must call upon the Lord quietly and without disturbance, so that our voice may not distract the senses and the attention of the mind and interrupt the prayer. When the mind gets used to this work, it will receive strength from the Spirit to pray vigorously and in all ways. Then there will be no need to say the prayer orally, and it will even be impossible. He who has attained to this will be fully satisfied with mental prayer."[2]

In recommending vocal prayer from time to time, St. Gregory combines his method with that of St. John of the

---

[1] Certain knowledge about Silence and Prayer : On how to obtain the action.

[2] Philokalia (Instructions to Hesychasts : How to say the Prayer).

Ladder. In substance it is the same rule; but St. Gregory speaks of it in his well-known degree of proficiency. He who diligently practises Climacus' method will in due time reach that state of prayer of which the Sinaite speaks. Prayer, according to the Sinaite's very sound and practical opinion, must be accompanied especially by patience or perseverance.

"The hesychast should mostly sit for the practice of prayer on account of the difficulty of this labour, and sometimes for a short time he may even lie on his bed in order to give the body some respite. Your sitting should be in patience, to fulfil the command that we must *persevere in prayer* (Col. 4: 2) and not soon stop and give up on account of the extremely heavy labour of the mental invocation and the constant immersion of the mind in the heart. Thus the Prophet says: *Pains have seized me like those in travail* (Jer. 8: 21). But bend your head down, and gather your mind into your heart—if your heart has opened to you— and invoke the help of the Lord Jesus. Feeling pain in the shoulders and often afflicted with headache, endure this with perseverance and zeal, and seek the Lord in your heart. For the kingdom of heaven is the inheritance of those who force themselves, and those who force themselves *capture it* (Matt. 11: 12). The Lord has shown that true diligence consists in the endurance of these and similar pains. Patience and waiting in every activity is the parent of pains of body and soul."[1]

The word pain here mostly means contrition of spirit, the weeping or mourning of the spirit, its pain and suffering from the realization of its sinfulness, from the realization of eternal death, from the realization of its slavery to

---

[1] How the Hesychast should Sit and Make the Prayer.

fallen spirits. The suffering of the spirit is communicated to the heart and the body, as they are inseparably bound up with the spirit in such a way that there is a natural necessity for them to participate in its states. For those who are weak physically contrition of spirit, weeping and mourning fully takes the place of bodily toil.[1] But for people of strong constitution the discipline of the body is indispensable; in their case without the discipline of the body the heart will not acquire that blessed peace which is born in the weak from the realization and recognition of their weakness.

"No bodily or spiritual activity," says St. Gregory, "without pain or toil ever brings fruit to him who practises it, because *the kingdom of heaven is taken by force, and the forceful capture it* (Matt. 11: 12). By *force* understand a sense of bodily pain in all you do. Many have laboured for many years and still labour painlessly, yet because they have no patience for toil or fervour of heart for pain, they fail to acquire purity and the Holy Spirit through their refusal of the austerity of pain. For those who work carelessly and slackly apparently toil greatly, but they never gather fruit because they take no pains and are fundamentally painless. A witness to this is he who says: 'Whatever great struggles we may have endured, if we have not acquired a suffering heart they are counterfeit and useless.'[2] The great St. Ephrem testifies to the same thing, saying: 'While toiling toil painfully, in order to avoid the painfulness of vain labours. For if, according to the Prophet, our loins are not filled with the pain of fasting, and if pangs do not take hold of us as the pangs of a woman in travail, we shall not con-

---

[1] St. Isaac the Syrian, ch. 89.

[2] Ladder: 7: 64.

ceive the Spirit of salvation on the earth of our heart (Is.
21: 3; 26: 18). Let us not merely boast of our living in
a barren desert and of our idle quiet, thinking ourselves to
be something on this account. At the time of our departure
(death), we shall all know for certain the whole fruit of our
life."[1]

The teaching of St. Gregory the Sinaite on the painfulness
which accompanies the true activity of a hesychast's mental
prayer, may seem strange, as it *has* seemed strange, to the
carnal and natural mind unacquainted practically with the
monastic life. We invite such people to turn their attention
to the evidence obtained by experience, and we testify that
not only the activity of mental prayer but even the attentive
reading of deep patristic writings on the subject will produce
headache. Contrition of heart on account of one's sinfulness, slavery and death revealed by prayer is so powerful
that it will produce in the body pains and sufferings the very
existence of which, and even the possibility of their existence, is quite unknown to those unacquainted with the
labour of prayer. When the heart confesses to the Lord its
sinfulness and its wretched state, then the body is crucified.
I have suffered, says David, experienced in the labour of
prayer, *and been utterly bent. I walked sorrowing all
day long. For my loins are filled with illusions, and there
is no healing in my flesh. I have been afflicted and humbled
exceedingly. I roared from the groaning of my heart* (Ps.
37: 7-9).

What is particularly remarkable in the teaching of St.
Gregory is that he insists that the mind must concentrate on
the heart. This is what the Fathers call the artistic activity
of prayer, which they forbid to beginners, both monks and

---

[1] On Quiet and Prayer (Philokalia) : par. 14.

laymen, who need considerable preparatory training. And even prepared monks must approach this artistic activity with the greatest reverence, fear of God and caution. In ordering that the mind should be concentrated on the heart, the Saint adds: *If your heart has opened.* This means that the union of the mind with the heart is a gift of divine grace, granted in its time at God's discretion, but not at any time and not at the discretion of the ascetic. The gift of attentive prayer is usually preceded by special sufferings and upheavals of the soul which lead our spirit down into the depth of the realization of its poverty and nothingness.[1] The gift of God is attracted by humility and fidelity to God expressed by the resolute rejection of all sinful thoughts at their very appearance. Fidelity is a cause of purity. To purity and humility are entrusted the gifts of the Spirit.[2]

ST. NICEPHORUS OF MOUNT ATHOS.

The artistic activity of mental prayer is explained with special clarity and fulness by blessed Nicephorus, a monk who practised silence on holy Mount Athos. He rightly calls this work of prayer the art of arts and science of sciences since it provides the mind and heart with knowledge and impressions which are infused directly by the Spirit of God, whereas all other sciences supply merely human knowledge and impressions. Mental activity is the highest school of theology.

"This greatest of great activities," says the great director of hesychasts, "is acquired by many, or even all, through

---

[1] St. Isaac the Syrian, ch. 78.
[2] Luke 16 : 10-12.

learning. Occasionally without learning people receive it from God by strenuous labour and warmth of faith; but this is an exception, not the rule. Therefore it is necessary to look for an undeluded director in order to learn from his instruction to distinguish the right and left deficiencies and superfluities in the work of attention that are due to the instigation of the evil one. From the very fact that the director has suffered and been tempted himself, he will be able to explain to us what is required and will truly show us this spiritual way, which we shall therefore easily accomplish. If there is no director at hand, we must seek him without regretting the labour. But if after such a search he is not to be found, after calling upon God in contrition of spirit and with tears, and after praying to Him earnestly with humility, do what I tell you.

"You are aware that our breathing by which we live is an inhaling and exhaling of air. The organs that serve for this purpose are the lungs which surround the heart. They pass air through themselves and flood the heart with it. Thus breathing is the natural way to the heart. And so, collect your mind and conduct it by way of your breathing by which air passes to the heart and together with the inhaled air force it to descend into the heart and to stay there. And train it not to come out of there quickly; for at first this inner enclosure and restraint is very wearisome, but when it becomes accustomed to it, then on the contrary it does not like whirling without, because it is there filled with joy and happiness. Just as when a man who has been away from home returns, he forgets himself for joy that he is again with his wife and children, embraces them and cannot stop talking to them—so too the mind, when it is united to the heart, is filled with unutterable joy and sweetness. Then it sees that the kingdom of heaven is truly within us, for it now sees it within itself. And as it seeks with pure prayer to stay and be strengthened in it, it regards all outward things as repulsive and hateful.

"When you enter the place of the heart as I have shown you, give thanks to God and, while glorifying His goodness, always maintain this activity; it will teach you what you will never learn in any other way. And you should also know that when your mind is established in the heart, it must not remain there silent and idle, but must unceasingly make the prayer: *Lord Jesus Christ, Son of God, have mercy on me!* This prayer, by holding the mind without dreaming, renders it inaccessible and immune to the appeals of the enemy and daily leads it more and more into love and longing for God.

"But if after labouring much, brother, you cannot enter the domain of the heart as I have told you, do as I shall further tell you, and with God's help you will find what you are seeking. You are aware that the power of speech (or the reasoning faculty) is located in the breast. For within the breast, when our mouth is silent, we speak, deliberate, say prayers, sing psalms, and so on. And so, having driven out of it every thought (for you can if you want to), make this faculty of speech say: *Lord Jesus Christ, Son of God, have mercy on me!* And force it to cry within the breast instead of any other thought only this. If you do this for some time the entry into the heart will be opened to you without any doubt, as I have already written, having learnt it from experience. And with much yearning and sweet attention there will also come to you a whole host of virtues: love, joy, peace and the rest, on account of which your every wish will be fulfilled through Jesus Christ our Lord."[1]

Here in the first place we should notice the spirituality[2] of the blessed Father and the spirituality[2] which he saw in the monk whom he was instructing. This may be seen in the sections of his article which precede the exposition of the art. There it is evident from the reference to the life of St. Saba that the teaching on silence of the heart for which and in connection with which outward silence of the body is procured, is suitable for those monks who have been fully trained in the rules of the monastic life, can struggle with opposing thoughts and keep watch over their mind.

To the person he is instructing St. Nicephorus says: "You are aware that the power of speech[3] is located in the breast. For within the breast, when the mouth is silent, we speak, deliberate, say prayers, sing psalms and so on." Very few have a clear sense of the power of speech[3] in their breast so as to be able to pray and sing psalms in their heart. This is the gift of those who have made considerable progress, who have practised the prayer for a long time according to the method of St. John of the Ladder, who have acquired a considerable degree of concentration and by very attentive prayer have aroused their spirit (here called speech[3]) to abundant sympathy with the mind. In people in their ordinary state, the spirit, struck by the fall, sleeps an unwakable sleep identical with death. It is incapable of the spiritual exercises indicated here and awakes for them only when the mind is constantly and persistently

---

[1] Philokalia, Profitable Discourse on Sobriety or Vigilance.

[2] Or : adornment, spiritual development or level.

[3] Speech. The word may also mean "reasoning faculty."

occupied in rousing it by means of the lifegiving name of Jesus.

The method suggested by S. Nicephorus is excellent. In his exposition of it, for one who understands the matter it is clear that one must prepare for it gradually, and at the same time that its acquisition is the gift of God. As this method is explained in particular detail in the works of Xanthopoulos on prayer and silence, we shall pass to his writings.

ST. KALLISTUS XANTHOPOULOS.

St. Kallistus Xanthopoulos was a disciple of St. Gregory the Sinaite and spent his monastic life on Mount Athos. He was first trained for the monastic life in a community. Later, when he seemed ready for it, he passed to the life of a hesychast. He learnt mental prayer while in obedience to the cook of the monastery. He also had secular learning. This may be clearly seen from the books written by him. Towards the end of his life he was raised to the rank of Patriarch of Constantinople. St. Ignatius was his closest friend and the sharer of his monastic labours. Both attained great proficiency in prayer. Their book was written exclusively for hesychasts. To the technique expounded by St. Nicephorus they add that in using it *the mouth should be closed*. They say that a beginner in the hesychast life should practise the prayer of Jesus by the method of St. Nicephorus and unceasingly lead it into the heart *gently* by means of breathing through the nose, and that one should exhale equally gently, keeping the mouth shut.[1]

---

[1] Chaps. 19 and 45.

It is very important to know the significance which the holy teachers of mental prayer give to the technique offered by them which, being a material aid, must on no account be confused with the actual operation of the prayer, and to which no special importance should be attached as if all the success of the prayer depended upon it. In the success of prayer it is the power and grace of God that is the efficient cause and that accomplishes everything. The aids remain aids required by our weakness, and are rejected as unneeded and superfluous when success is obtained. To put one's hope and trust in these aids is very dangerous, for it leads to a wrong, material conception of prayer and diverts one from a spiritual understanding of it which is the only true one. A false understanding or conception of prayer always leads to a fruitless or harmful practice of it.

"And so, know, brother," say Sts. Kallistus and Ignatius, "that every art and every rule and, if you wish, every different form of activity is prescribed and rightly appointed for the simple reason that we cannot yet pray in our heart purely and undistractedly. But when this is accomplished by the will and grace of our Lord Jesus Christ, then we abandon the many and diverse and varied, and we are united immediately and ineffably with the One, the Single and the Unifying.[1] By remaining in the art of the pure and undistracted prayer of the heart as explained above—but it can be partly impure and not free from distraction, apparently on account of the thoughts and memories of the past which rise up and hinder it[2]—the ascetic gradually learns to pray without having to force himself and without wandering, purely and truly; that is, he reaches a state in which the

---

[1] Ch. 38.

[2] The words in parentheses are by Brianchaninov.

mind remains in the heart and is not merely led into it under compulsion and occasionally by way of the breathing, and then jumps out again, but it remains there constantly and prays without ceasing."[1]

The labour of mental prayer of the heart is "accomplished by the mind through its overshadowing with the help of divine grace and through the single-thought,[2] heartfelt, pure, unwandering invocation with faith of our Lord Jesus Christ, and not through the one, mere, natural art of breathing through the nose, or through sitting in a quiet and dark place when practising the prayer—God forbid! This was invented by the Divine Fathers merely as a help to collecting the mind from its usual wandering and to restoring it to itself and to attention.[3] Before all spiritual gifts undistraction (concentration) is given to the mind by our Lord Jesus Christ and the invocation in the heart of His holy name with faith. This is assisted to some extent by a natural art which aids the leading down of the mind into the heart by means of breathing through the nose. Sitting in a quiet and darkish place is also helpful, and other aids of this kind."[4]

Sts. Kallistus and Ignatius strictly forbid all premature striving for what, according to the spiritual system of the monastic life, has its own appointed time. They wish a monk to act in the order appointed for him, according to the laws taught by divine grace. "And you," they say, "who desire to learn the silence that leads to heaven, wisely follow the appointed laws, and in the first place embrace obedience

---

[1] Ch. 53.
[2] A technical term.
[3] Ch. 24.
[4] Heading of Ch. 24.

gladly, then silence. Just as action is a step to contemplation, so obedience is the portico to silence. *Pass not beyond
the ancient bounds which thy fathers have set,* says Scripture (Prov. 22: 28). *Woe to him that is alone* (Eccles.
4: 10). Thus having first laid a good foundation, you will
be able eventually to put a most glorious roof on the Spirit's
architecture. Just as all is rejected when the beginning is
unskilful, so on the contrary when the beginning is skilled
all is beautiful, although the opposite also sometimes
happens."[1]

It is generally recognized that until the acquisition of
concentration that is not illusory or brief but constant and
real, it is useful to practise the prayer of Jesus in monastic
company, while furthering the practice of the prayer with
the practical carrying out of the commandments of the
Gospel, or with what amounts to the same thing, humility.
After receiving the gift of concentration it is permitted to
undertake silence. That is how Saints Basil the Great and
Gregory the Theologian acted. According to St. Isaac the
Syrian they at first occupied themselves with the fulfilment
of those commandments which concern people living in
human society, and practised prayer that corresponded to
that state. From this life their mind began to feel stillness
and concentration. Then they withdrew into the solitude
of the desert, where they engaged in activity in the inner
man, and attained contemplation.[2]

To practise perfect silence in our time is very difficult,
almost impossible. Saraphim of Sarov, Ignatius
Nikiforovsky, and Nikander Babaevsky, monks who were
extremely proficient in mental prayer, lived sometimes in

---

[1] Ch. 14.
[2] St. Isaac the Syrian, Ch. 55.

silence and sometimes in community. The last in particular never withdrew into silence perceptible to men, though in soul he was a great hesychast.

The way of silence by which St. Arsenius the Great was directed has always been excellent, and now must be acknowledged to be the best. This Father constantly observed silence, did not go to the brothers' cells, received visitors into his own cell only in cases of extreme necessity, stood in church somewhere behind a column, did not write and did not receive letters, in general withdrew from all contacts that could disturb his attention, and had as the aim of his life and all his actions the preservation of attention.[1] The way of life and silence by which St. Arsenius attained great proficiency is highly praised and recommended for imitation by St. Isaac the Syrian as an extremely easy, wise and fruitful way.[2]

As a conclusion to our extracts from the works of Sts. Kallistus and Ignatius, let us quote their experienced opinion, which agrees with the opinion of other holy Fathers, that to acquire unwandering prayer of the heart much time and much effort are needed. "To pray constantly within the heart," they say, "and even higher states than that, are attained not simply, as if by chance, not by means of a little labour and time, though even that occurs occasionally by the inscrutable providence of God; but it requires a long time, and no little labour, a struggle of body and soul, much and prolonged exertion. On account of the excellence·of the gift and the grace of which we hope to partake, there must be, according to our power, equal and

---

[1] Alphabetical Patrology and Memorable Sayings of St. Arsenius the Great.

[2] St. Isaac the Syrian, ch. 41

corresponding labours, in order that, according to the mystical and sacred doctrine, the enemy may be expelled from the ranges of the heart and Christ may be manifestly instated there. Says St. Isaac: 'Let him who wishes to see the Lord endeavour artistically to purify his heart with the remembrance of God. And in this manner, by the clarity of his thought he will hourly see the Lord.' And St. Barsanouphius: 'If interior activity by the grace of God does not help a man, he will labour in vain exteriorly. Interior activity combined with anguish of heart brings purity, and purity brings true silence of the heart. By such silence humility is secured, and humility makes a man a dwelling of God. But when God dwells in a man, then the demons and passions are driven out, and the man becomes a temple of God, filled with sanctification, filled with illumination, purity and grace. Blessed is he who sees the Lord in the innermost treasury of his heart as in a mirror, and with weeping pours out his prayer before His goodness.' St. John Karpathios: 'Much time and labour in prayer is necessary in order to find in poise of mind another heaven of the heart where Christ dwells, as the Apostle says: *Do you not know that Jesus Christ is in you? Unless indeed you are failures!* ' (2 Cor. 13: 5)."[1]

MATERIAL AIDS.

With these excerpts from the holy Fathers we shall content ourselves, since they satisfactorily explain the work of the prayer of Jesus. In the other patristic writings the same teaching is given. We consider it necessary for our

[1] Ch. 52.

beloved fathers and brethren to repeat the warning that
they should not be in a hurry to read the writings of the
Fathers on the most exalted monastic states and activities,
though love of knowledge draws one to such reading, though
such reading produces ecstasy and delight. Our freedom,
according to the nature of the time, must be particularly
limited. When there were spiritual directors, then the
attachments of beginners were easily noticed and cured.
But now there is no one to cure or even to notice the attachments. Often a pernicious attachment is taken for great
progress by inexperienced directors; the attached person is
spurred on to greater attachment. An attachment which
has started to act on a monk without being noticed, continues to act and to draw him further and further from the
true course. It will be no mistake to say that the majority
of people have some kind of attachment; those who have
renounced their attachment or attachments are very few,
while people who have never been attached simply do not
exist. Therefore, now that the patristic books have become
our sole means of direction, we should read them with
special care and caution lest our one means of direction
should be turned into a source of wrong activity and the
confusion that results from it.

"Let us seek," says St. John of the Ladder concerning
the choice of a director, "not such as have the gift of fore-
knowledge and spiritual insight, but rather such as are
unquestionably humble and whose character and place of
residence correspond to our maladies."[1]

The same must be said about books too, as we have
already said above. We should on no account choose the
most exalted and sublime, but rather those that are near to

---

[1] Ladder of Paradise : 4 : 121.

our state and which explain the activity proper for us. "It is a great evil," said St. Isaac the Syrian, "to teach some high doctrine to one who is still in the rank of beginners and in spiritual stature is still an infant."[1]

The carnal and natural man, on hearing spiritual guidance, understands it in conformity with his state, twists and distorts it, and by following it in his distorted sense, takes a wrong course and holds to it stubbornly as a course given by holy guidance. A certain elder reached Christian perfection by the special providence of God after entering silence, contrary to the rules, in his youth. At first he lived in silence in a forest in Russia, living in a mud-hut, and afterwards on Mount Athos. After his return to Russia he lived in a community in an unsubsidized monastery. Seeing in the elder the undoubted signs of sanctity, many of the brethren went to him for advice. The elder gave instructions from his own experience and did harm to the souls of the brethren. A monk who knew the elder well said to him:

"Father! You speak to the brothers about activities and states which are beyond their understanding and experience. The result is that they interpret your words in their own way, and by acting in accordance with that interpretation, they do themselves harm."

The elder replied with holy simplicity: "I see that myself! But what am I to do? I regard all as higher than myself, and when they ask I reply from my own experience (lit. state)."

The common or general monastic way was unknown to the elder. Not only sin is fatal for us, but good is also fatal when we do it not at the proper time or not in due

[1] Ch. 74.

measure. Thus not only is a famine fatal, but also excess of food or a quality of food that does not suit our age or constitution. *Neither is new wine put into old wineskins; if it is, the skins burst, and the wine is spilled, and the skins are ruined; but new wine is put into fresh wineskins, and so both are preserved.*[1] The Lord said this of the acts of virtue which must unfailingly agree with the state of the doer. Otherwise they will ruin the doer and will perish themselves; that is, they will be undertaken fruitlessly and will harm and ruin the soul, which is the exact opposite of their purpose.

Besides the aids explained above, for the assistance of beginners in the practice of the prayer of Jesus there are also various other aids. We shall enumerate the chief of them.

1. A rosary or ladder.[2] A rosary usually consists of a hundred pips or beads, while a ladder[2] consists of a hundred steps, since in the rule performed with the prayer of Jesus the prayers are usually counted by the hundred. The rosary is used to count prostrations, and also monks sit and practise the prayer of Jesus at first by the rosary. But when through prayer attention increases, it becomes impossible to pray by a rosary and count the prayers. Then the whole attention is absorbed in the prayer.

2. It is very useful to train oneself to the prayer of Jesus by performing it with prostrations and bows to the waist, making them unhurriedly and with a sense of penitence, as the blessed youth George made them, of whom St. Symeon the New Theologian tells in his article on faith.[3]

---

[1] Matt. 9 : 17.

[2] A kind of leather rosary with steps for beads, like a ladder by which we climb to heaven.

[3] Philokalia.

3. In church and in fact generally when practising the prayer of Jesus it is useful to keep the eyes closed.

4. It is also helpful to hold the left hand on the chest, over the left nipple of the breast, a little above it. This technique helps one to feel the power of speech which is in the breast.

5. The Fathers advise hesychasts to have a somewhat dark room or cell, with curtained windows, to keep the mind from distraction and to assist it to concentrate in the heart.

6. Hesychasts are advised to sit on a low stool, firstly because attentive prayer requires a restful position, and secondly after the example of the blind beggar mentioned in the Gospel who sat on the roadside and cried to the Lord, *Jesus, Son of David, have mercy on me* (Mk. 10: 47), and was heard and healed. Also this low stool represents the dunghill on which Job sat outside the city, when the devil struck him from head to foot with a terrible disease (Job 2: 8). A monk should see himself crippled, deformed, torn by sinfulness, cast out of his natural state by it, cast down to what is unnatural, and from his wretched state he should cry to the all-merciful and almighty Jesus, the Renewer of human nature; *Have mercy on me.* The low stool is very convenient for the practice of the prayer of Jesus. This does not mean that standing is banned, but as nearly all the time of a true hesychast is devoted to prayer, he is allowed to engage in it sitting down, and sometimes even in a lying posture. Especially the sick and elderly should beware of excessive bodily exertion so as not to exhaust their powers and make it impossible for them to engage in spiritual labour. The essence of the work is in the Lord and in His name. The paralytic was let down on his bed before the Lord through the roof of the house, and

received healing. Healing is attracted by faith and humility.

7. Those who practise mental activity sometimes have to pour cold water on themselves or apply towels soaked in water to the places where there is blood-congestion. The water should be at summer temperature, and on no account very cold as the latter only increases the heat. Generally speaking mental occupations tend to produce fever in certain constitutions. Abba Dorotheus felt a fever of this kind when he was studying science, and that is why he cooled himself with water.[1] Fever of this kind must certainly be felt by those who force themselves much to the union of the mind with the heart by means of material aids and give them excessive importance, and fail to give due importance to spiritual aids.

In the case of special material exertion to acquire the prayer of the heart, a warmth begins to act in the heart. This warmth is the direct result of such an effort. Every member of the human body that is subjected to friction gets heated. The same thing happens in the case of the heart under long and constant strain. The warmth which appears as a result of vigorous, meterial exertion is also material. It is a warmth of the flesh and blood, in the realm of our fallen nature. An inexperienced ascetic, on feeling this warmth, will unfailingly think it is something wonderful, and will take pleasure and delight in it; and that is the beginning of self-deception. Not only should we not think anything special of this warmth, but on the contrary we should take special precautionary measures as soon as it makes its appearance. Precaution is necessary because this

---

[1] Holy Abba Dorotheus. Meditation 10 : "How to go on the Way to God."

warmth, being of the blood, not only passes to different places in the breast, but can also very easily drop to the lower parts of the stomach and cause there the most violent excitement and burning. It is natural that carnal desire should then begin to act, for that is characteristic of those parts in a state of excitement. Some who have reached this state and have not understood what was happening to them, have given way to confusion, to despondency, to despair, as is known from experience. Regarding their state as desperate, they had recourse to famous elders and sought in their advice a cure for their souls, tortured with doubt and misery. Hearing that at the invocation of the name of Jesus there had appeared the most violent burning combined with the action of lust, the elders were horrified at the devil's wiles. They saw here a terrible delusion. They ordered the sufferers to stop the practice of the prayer of Jesus as the cause of this evil. They told many other ascetics about this phenomenon, as a remarkable and disastrous consequence of the practice of the prayer of Jesus. And many believed their judgment out of respect for the elder's renowned name; they believed that their judgment was the fruit of actual experience.

Actually this terrible delusion is merely a congestion of the blood brought about by a violent, ignorant use of material aids. This congestion can be easily cured in two or three days by applying to the inflamed parts linen soaked in summer water.

Far more dangerous, far nearer to delusion is it when the ascetic feels this natural[1] warmth in his heart or breast and takes it for a gift of grace, thinks of it and therefore

---

[1] Lit. "blood."

of himself as something, begins to imagine[1] delight for himself, to darken, deceive, enmesh, ruin himself with conceit. The more bodily exertion and effort an ascetic makes, the more violently the warmth of the blood is increased. And so it ought to be! In order to moderate this warmth and prevent its falling down, no special effort should be made to press the mind into the heart, the heart should not be overworked, and heat should not be produced by excessive holding of the breath and straining of the heart. On the contrary, the breathing must be checked gently, and the mind must be led into union with the heart very gently. We should try to ensure that the prayer acts in the very summit of the heart where the power of speech resides according to the teaching of the Fathers, and where divine worship should therefore be performed.

When divine grace overshadows the labour of prayer and begins to unite the mind with the heart, then material blood warmth completely vanishes. Then the sacred action of prayer undergoes a great change. It becomes as it were natural, perfectly light and free. Then there appears in the heart another warmth, subtle, immaterial, spiritual, which does not produce any excitement or burning. On the contrary, it cools, illumines, bedews, refreshes, and acts as a healing, spiritual, soothing unction; and it induces unutterable love for God and men. That is what St. Maximus Kapsokalivitis says of this warmth from his own blessed experience.[2]

---

[1] Or, fabricate.
[2] Philokalia.

THE DANGER OF DELUSION.

I offer fathers and brothers my poor advice, begging them not to reject my poor advice. Do not force yourself prematurely to the discovery within yourself of the action of the prayer of the heart. Prudent caution is most necessary, especially in our time when it is almost impossible to find a satisfactory guide in these matters, when the ascetic must himself force his way gropingly by the direction of the writings of the holy Fathers to the treasury of spiritual knowledge, and also must gropingly select for himself what is suited to his needs. While living according to the commandments of the Gospel, attentively practise the prayer of Jesus according to the method of St. John of the Ladder, combining prayer with weeping, having as the beginning and end of prayer repentance. In its own time, known to God, the action of the prayer of the heart will be revealed of itself. Such action, revealed by the touch of the finger of God, is more excellent than that which is acquired by vigorously forcing oneself by means of material aids. It is more excellent in many respects. It is far more extensive and voluminous, far more abundant. It is quite safe from delusion and other dangers. He who receives in this way sees in what he receives only the mercy of God, a gift of God, while he who attains by the vigorous use of material aids, though seeing the gift of God, he cannot fail to see his own effort and labour, he cannot fail to see his own mechanical aid which he has used, he cannot fail to ascribe to it special importance. This on the subtle way of the spirit is a considerable defect, a considerable obstacle, a considerable hindrance to the development of spiritual proficiency. For the development of spiritual proficiency there is no

G

end, no limits. An insignificant, unnoticed hope or trust in something outside God can stop the advance of progress and proficiency, in which faith in God is leader, guide, legs and wings. "Christ for the believer is all," said St. Mark.[1]

Of those who have used with special diligence the material aids very few have attained success, but very many have deranged and harmed themselves. With an experienced director the use of the material aids incurs little danger; but with the guidance of books it is very dangerous since it is so easy, through ignorance and imprudence, to fall into delusion and other kinds of spiritual and bodily disorder. Thus some, on seeing the harmful consequences of indiscreet labour and having only a superficial and confused idea of the prayer of Jesus and the circumstances that accompany it, attributed these consequences not to ignorance and imprudence but to the most holy prayer of Jesus itself. Can anything be sadder and more disastrous than this blasphemy, this delusion?

In teaching the prayer of the heart the holy Fathers did not say exactly in which part of the heart it ought to be performed, probably because in those times there was no need for such instruction. St. Nicephorus says, as of something well-known, that the power of speech is located in the breast and that when this faculty is aroused to participation in the prayer, the heart is also aroused to such participation. It is difficult for those who know something thoroughly in all its details to foresee and anticipate with a solution all the questions and problems that may arise from complete ignorance. Where ignorance sees darkness, knowledge finds nothing obscure. In later times a vague reference to the heart in the patristic writings caused great

---

[1] Spiritual Law : Ch. 4.

perplexity and a wrong practice of prayer in those who without a director and without studying with due care the writings of the Fathers, on the basis of superficial ideas snatched from a hasty reading, decided to engage in the artistic prayer of the heart, putting all their hope and trust in the material aids to its practice. A definite explanation of this subject has therefore become indispensable.

The human heart has the shape of an oblong bag which widens upwards and narrows towards the base. It is fastened by its upper extremity which is opposite the left nipple of the breast, but its lower part which descends towards the end of the ribs is free; when shaken, this shaking is called the beating of the heart. Many, having no idea of the arrangement of the heart, think that their heart is where they feel its beating. In undertaking on their own the practice of the prayer of the heart and in trying to lead their breathing into their heart, they direct it to just that part of the heart and cause carnal excitement there. Then when this greatly increases the beating of the heart they invite it to themselves and thrust on themselves a wrong state and delusion. The monk Basil and the elder Païssy Velitchkovsky say that many of their contemporaries harmed themselves by misusing material aids. And in later times cases of derangement caused in this way were frequently met. In fact they are met even now, although the disposition to practise the prayer of Jesus has decreased almost to vanishing point. One is bound to meet them. They are the inevitable consequence of ignorant, self-directed, conceited, premature and proud zeal, and finally of a complete lack of experienced directors.

The monk Basil, referring to St. Theophylact and other Fathers, affirms that the three powers of the soul, the power of speech (or reason), the power of fervour and the power of desire are disposed thus: the power of speech (reason), or the spirit of the man is present in the breast and in the upper part of the heart; the power of fervour in the middle part; and the power of desire or natural cupidity in the lower part. He who tries to set in motion and warm the lower part of the heart, sets in motion the power of cupidity which, on account of the nearness to it of the sexual parts and on account of their nature, sets in motion those parts. The most violent burning of carnal desire follows an ignorant use of a material aid. What a strange phenomenon! An ascetic apparently engages in prayer, but the occupation produces lust which it ought to mortify. And ignorance, having misused a material aid, ascribes to the prayer of Jesus what it ought to ascribe to misuse.

The prayer of the heart springs from the union of the mind with the spirit which were separated by the fall and are united by the grace of redemption. In the human spirit are concentrated feelings of conscience, humility, meekness, love for God and one's neighbour, and other similar properties. During prayer the action of these properties needs to be united with the action of the mind. All one's attention should be directed to this end. This union is affected by the finger of God Who alone can heal the wound of the fall. But the practiser of prayer shows the sincerity of his will to receive healing by his constant perseverance in prayer, by shutting his mind in the words of the prayer, and by exterior and interior activity according to the commandments of the Gospel, which render the spirit capable of union with the mind of the person praying. In addition to this the artistic direction of the mind towards the seat of speech in the upper part of the heart helps to some extent. Generally speaking, excessive exertion in the use of this material aid is harmful as it arouses material warmth. Warmth of flesh and blood should have no place in prayer.

On account of its soul-saving effect upon us of prayer in general, and of the remembrance of God or the prayer of Jesus in particular, as means to remaining in constant union with God and to constantly repulsing the attacks of the enemy, engagement in the prayer of Jesus is especially hateful to the devil. Those who pray in the name of the Lord Jesus are liable to special persecution by the devil. "All the labour and all the care of our adversary," says St. Makarius the Great, "consists in trying to divert our thought from the remembrance of God and from love for Him. To this end he uses the charm of the world, and draws us away from the true good to false, unreal goods."[1] Therefore he who has consecrated himself to the true service of God must specially guard himself against letting his thoughts wander by the unceasing prayer of Jesus and must on no account allow himself to be mentally idle. Without paying any attention to the thoughts and images that make their appearance, he must constantly return to prayer by the name of Jesus as to a harbour or haven, believing that Jesus indefatigably takes care of that servant of His who keeps near Him constantly by the unwearying remembrance of Him.

"The wicked demons," says St. Nilus the Sinaite, "*at night* try to disturb the spiritual workers themselves, but *during the day* they do so through men by surrounding him with calumnies, adversities and mishaps."[2] This order in the satanic struggle is soon observed in actual experience

[1] Word 1 : 3 ; Word 2 : 15.
[2] On Prayer : Ch. 139 (Philokalia).

by every practiser of prayer. The demons tempt by
thoughts, by mental images, by the remembrance of the most
needed objects, by reflections on apparently spiritual subjects, by arousing anxiety and worry and various fears and
apprehensions, and by other manifestations of unbelief.
In all the varied conflicts of the demons, a sense of disturbance or agitation always serves as a true sign of the
approach of fallen spirits, even though the action produced
by them has an appearance of justice. To ascetics living
in solitude and praying vigorously, devils appear in the
form of monsters, in the form of tempting objects, sometimes in the form of radiant angels, martyrs, saints and even
Christ Himself. One should not fear the threats of the
devils, and towards all apparitions in general one should
maintain an attitude of extreme incredulity. In such cases,
which however are rare, our foremost duty is to have recourse to God, to surrender ourselves wholly to His will
and to ask for His help. We should pay no attention to the
apparitions and not enter into relations or conversation with
them, regarding ourselves as unfit to deal with hostile spirits
and unworthy to converse with holy spirits.

HUMAN OPPOSITION.

A true, God-pleasing ascetic of prayer is liable to special
afflictions and persecutions from his fellow men. And in
this, as we have already said, the chief actors are demons.
They use as their tools those persons who have made their
activity one with the activity of the demons, and also those
who do not understand the fiendish conflicts and therefore
easily become the devils' tools, and even those who under-

stand the enemy's cunning but are not careful enough or attentive to themselves and so let themselves be deceived. The most striking and horrible example of the terrible hatred for God, for the Word of God and for the Spirit of God with which men can be infected whose spirit and outlook has become one with that of the demons we see in the Jewish high priests, elders, scribes and Pharisees who committed the greatest of all human crimes—Deicide.[1] St. Symeon the New Theologian says that, by the instigation of devils, monks leading an insincere life envy true ascetics and do all in their power to disconcert them or expel them from the community. Even well-intentioned monks who however live an outward life and have no conception of the interior life, take offence at spiritual workers, consider their conduct strange, condemn and slander them, and insult and persecute them in various ways. A great practiser of the prayer of Jesus, the blessed elder Seraphim of Sarov, suffered through the ignorance of his brother monks and their carnal view of monasticism, because those who read the Law of God bodily think they can fulfil it with outward actions alone without spiritual labour, *not understanding either what they are saying or the things about which they make assertions* (1 Tim. 1: 7).[2]

"In following the way of the interior, contemplative life," St. Seraphim instructs and comforts us, drawing the instruction and comfort from his own spiritual experience, "we must not give in and abandon it because people who are attached to what is outward and sensible oppose our heart's most cherished convictions with their opinions and do all they can to divert us from living an interior life by putting

---

[1] The murder of the God-man, Jesus Christ.
[2] St. Mark the Ascetic : "Spiritual Law," Ch. 34.

all kinds of obstacles in our way. No opposition must
deter us from going this way, but we must take our stand
on the word of God: *We shall not fear their fear nor be
alarmed, for God is with us. We shall sanctify the Lord our
God* by the heartfelt remembrance of His divine name, *and
He shall be our fear*" (Is. 8: 10-13).[1]

When St. Gregory the Sinaite (Divine Providence used
him in the 14th century as an instrument for the revival of
mental prayer among monks) arrived on Mount Athos and
began to share his God-given knowledge with pious ascetics
who were fervent and intelligent but understood the service
of God only in a bodily manner, at first they strongly opposed him—so strange does the doctrine of spiritual labour
seem to those who have no idea of it and are unaware of
its existence, and who give to bodily labour undue importance.
Still stranger does mental activity seem to the carnal and
natural mind, especially when it is infected with the blight
of conceit and the poison of heresy. Then the hatred of
the human spirit which has entered into alliance with satan
against the Spirit of God expresses itself with unnatural
fury. In order to make this clear and show in vivid relief
how pervertedly the carnal and natural mind understands
everything spiritual and distorts it to conform with the
darkness of the fall in which it gropes, despite its earthly
learning, we shall relate briefly here the slanders and
calumny against mental activity of the Latin monk Barlaam
and certain Western writers.

Bishop Innocent in his history of the Church says that
Barlaam, a Calabrian monk, in the 15th century arrived in
Salonika, a town of the Eastern Greek Empire. There, in
order to act on behalf of the Western Church under cover

---

[1] Instruction 29.

of Orthodoxy, he renounced Latinism. Having written several works to prove the rightness of the Eastern Church, he thereby won the praise and trust of the Emperor Kantakuzene. Realising that Greek monasticism was the mainstay of the Church, he wanted to weaken it and even crush it, so as to shake the whole Church. With this object he expressed a desire to live the strictest monastic life, and craftily persuaded an Athos hermit to reveal to him the artistic practice of the prayer of Jesus.

Having got what he wanted, but having understood what had been revealed to him in an absurd and superficial manner, Barlaam took for the unique essence of the matter a material aid which the Fathers, as we have seen, call merely a certain help, and spiritual visions for material visions seen only with the bodily eyes. This he reported to the emperor as a serious error. A council was convoked in Constantinople. St. Gregory Palamas, an Athos monk and a great practiser of mental prayer, entered into controversy with Barlaam and by the power of the grace of God defeated him. Barlaam and his blasphemies were anathematised. He returned to Calabria and Roman Catholicism. But many Greeks who were superficial Christians believed his doctrine and brought it to the West where his blasphemies and absurd calumnies were accepted as a confession of the truth.

The historian Fleury, in describing Barlaam's teaching, concentrates the whole activity of mental prayer in a material aid, and so distorts it. Fleury makes an extract on technique from St. Symeon the New Theologian's "Three Ways of Prayer" contained in the Philokalia and affirms that Symeon teaches that one should sit in a corner of one's cell, *direct one's eyes and the whole of one's thought towards the centre of the stomach, that is, towards the navel, hold one's breath even by the nose,* and so on. It would be hard to believe that the learned and talented Fleury had written such nonsense, if it did not appear for all to see on the pages of his history.[1]

Bergier, another extremely learned and talented author, says that Greek monks, through striving for contemplation, went mad and became fanatics. In order to reach a state of ecstasy, they fixed their eyes on their navel and held their breath; then they imagined they saw a gleaming light, and so on.[2] In distorting and ridiculing the way of prayer practised by true contemplatives, the Latins do not hesitate to ridicule states of grace produced by prayer, do not hesitate to ridicule the action of the Holy Spirit. Let us leave the libels and blasphemies of heretics to the judgment of God. With a feeling of sorrow and not of condemnation let us turn our attention away from such nonsense. Let us listen to what our blessed exponent of the prayer of Jesus, Seraphim of Sarov, says of the vision of the light of Christ.

"In order to receive and see *in one's heart* the light of Christ, we must withdraw ourselves as much as possible from visible objects. Having purified our soul by penitence, good works and faith in Him Who was crucified for us, we should close our bodily eyes and immerse our mind in our heart, where we should cry with the invocation of the name of our Lord Jesus Christ. Then according to the measure of his zeal and fervour of spirit for the Beloved a man finds delight in the name pronounced which arouses desire to seek higher enlightenment. When through this exercise the mind tarries

---

[1] Vol. VI, Book 95, Ch. 9.

[2] Dictionnaire Théologique par Bergier, Tome 4, Hesichistes.

in the heart, then there dawns the light of Christ which sanctifies the temple of the soul with its divine radiance, as the Prophet Malachi says: *To you who fear My name, the Sun of Righteousness shall arise* (Mal. 4: 2). This light is at the same time life, according to the word of the Gospel: *In Him was life, and the life was the light of men* (Jn. 1: 4)."[1]

From this it is clear that, contrary to the view of Barlaam and the Latins, this light is not material but spiritual, and that it opens the eyes of the soul and is seen by them, although it also acts on the bodily eyes, as it did in the case of the holy Apostle Paul (cp. Acts 9). St. Makarius the Great, in explaining in detail and with special clarity the doctrine of this light in his 7th Word, says that: "It is a substantial shining of the power of the Holy Spirit in the soul. Through this light all knowledge is revealed and God is truly known by the worthy and beloved soul."[2]

In agreement with St. Makarius are all the Holy Fathers who have learnt Christian perfection by experience and who have described it in their writings with a description as adequate as that indescribable mystery allows in the realm of matter. It is very useful to know that a fruit of pure unwandering prayer is the renewal of our nature, and that our renewed nature is adorned and endowed with gifts of divine grace. But the striving to acquire these gifts prematurely, a striving by which through the instigation of pride God's will for us is forestalled, is extremely harmful and leads only to delusion. It is for this reason that all the Fathers speak very briefly about the gifts of grace, but speak very fully on how to acquire pure prayer of which the

---

[1] Instruction 12.

[2] Word 7 : 23.

gifts of grace are fruits. The work of prayer requires assiduous training, but the graces of prayer[1] appear of themselves as properties of our renewed nature when, after its purification by penitence, that nature is sanctified by the overshadowing of the Spirit.

Païssy Velitchkovsky who lived at the end of the 18th century wrote a treatise on mental prayer to refute the blasphemies of a certain *earthly-minded* monk philosopher who lived on the Moshensky Mountains and was a contemporary of Païssy. "In our days," writes Païssy in a letter to the elder Theodosius, "a certain monk, an earthly-minded philosopher, seeing that some with zeal for this prayer though not according to knowledge fell into delusion through their independence[2] or the ignorant guidance of directors inexperienced in this prayer, instead of blaming the independence and unskilled direction, attacked and blasphemed this holy prayer and, incited by the devil, attacked it to such an extent that they far surpassed even the ancient thrice-cursed heretics Barlaam and Akindynos. Neither afraid of God nor ashamed of men, he fabricated fearful and shameful blasphemies against this holy prayer and against its devotees and practisers, blasphemies intolerable for the chaste human ear. Over and above that, he raised such a tremendous persecution against the advocates of this prayer that some of them left everything and fled to our country, and are living a God-pleasing life as solitaries here. But others, being feeble-minded, were driven to such madness by the depraved words of the philosopher that even those who had books of the Fathers with them, drowned them—as we heard—in a river by tying them to

---

[1] "Graces of Prayer." Lit. "gifts of grace."

[2] Or, self-will, self-direction.

a brick. His blasphemies made such an impression that some directors forbade the reading of the books of the Fathers under pain of being deprived of their blessing. Not content with oral blasphemy, the philosopher intended to publish his blasphemies in writing. Then, struck by the rod of God, he became blind. With that his anti-God campaigns came to an end."

However rich it may be in worldly wisdom, the carnal and natural mind always regards mental prayer very suspiciously and unsympathetically. It is a means of union of the human spirit with God, and therefore it is particularly strange and hateful for those who are content for their spirit to remain in the company of rejected and fallen spirits, hostile to God, who are unaware of their fall, who proclaim and exalt the fallen state as if it were a state of the highest progress and proficiency. *The word of the cross*, preached by the lips of the apostles to all men, *is to those who are perishing foolishness*. It remains foolishness when it is preached by the mind to the heart and to the whole being of the old man by prayer. But for those who are being saved *it is the power of God* (1 Cor. 1: 18). Greeks who have never known Christianity, and *Greeks* who have returned from Christianity to Hellenism, *seek* in conformity with their spirit *wisdom* in mental prayer, and find *foolishness*. But true Christians by the apparently weak and meaningless labour of mental prayer find *Christ, the power of God and the wisdom of God. For the folly of God is wiser than men, and the weakness of God is stronger than men* (1 Cor. 1: 22-25). It is not surprising that our learned men too who had no idea of mental prayer according to the tradition of the Orthodox Church and who had merely read about it in the works of western authors, repeated the blasphemies and nonsense of those authors.[1]

The spiritual friend of the elder Païssy Velitchkovsky mentions other monks of his day who rejected the practice of the prayer of Jesus for three reasons: first, because they considered this practice suitable only for holy and dispassionate people; secondly, on account of the complete lack of directors; thirdly, on account of the delusion which sometimes follows mental labour. The groundlessness of these arguments has been examined by us in its place.[2] Here it will be enough to say that those who reject the practice of mental prayer for these reasons, engage exclusively in vocal prayer without even so attaining due proficiency. By rejecting a practical knowledge of mental prayer, they cannot acquire in oral prayer due attention which is secured pre-eminently by mental prayer. Psalmody performed vocally and orally, without attention and with considerable distraction—inevitable in the case of bodily workers who do not keep watch over their mind—acts on the soul very feebly and superficially, and produces fruits corresponding to its action. Very often when it is performed with clockwork regularity and in great quantity, it gives birth to conceit and its consequences.

"Many," says Father Basil, "having no practical knowledge of mental activity, erroneously judge that mental activity is suitable only for dispassionate and holy men. For this reason from outward habit, they keep only to psalmody, troparions and canons, and doze in this merely outward prayer of theirs. They do not understand that the hymns and prayers that have been handed down to us by the

---

[1] Encyclopaedic Dictionary of Elderhood. Hesychasts. Cp. art. in Bergier's Dictionary of Theology.

[2] Ascetic Essays. Pt. 1, "Conversation of an Elder with his Disciple on the Prayer of Jesus."

Fathers are only for a time, on account of the weakness and childishness of our mind, so that by gradually training ourselves we may mount to the degree of mental activity, and not stay till our dying day merely in psalmody. What is even more childish is when we say (lit. read) with our mouth our outward prayer and are carried away by the joyful thought that we are doing something great, consoling ourselves merely with quantity and thereby nourishing the inner Pharisee!"[1]

PRAYER AND LIFE.

Let everyone who names the name of the Lord depart from iniquity (2 Tim. 2: 19), commands the Apostle. This command refers to all Christians, but it specially refers to those who intend to practise unceasing prayer by the name of the Lord Jesus. The most pure name of Jesus cannot tolerate to dwell in the midst of impurity. It requires that all impurity should be expelled and banished from the vessel of the soul. It enters the vessel according to the degree of its purity, and it at once begins to act in it and effect the further purification for which the man's own efforts were insufficient and which is needed if the vessel is to become a worthy receptacle for the spiritual treasure, a shrine for the most holy Name.

Let us avoid overeating and even satisfaction. Let us make our rule moderate, constant abstinence in food and drink. Let us deny ourselves the pleasure of tasty foods and drinks. Let us sleep sufficiently, but not excessively.

---

[1] Preface to the book of St. Gregory the Sinaite.

Let us renounce idle talking, laughter, jokes, scoffing. Let us put a stop to unnecessary visits and receptions of brothers in our cell under the pretext of love, under which name are screened idle talks and occupations which devastate the soul. Let us renounce day-dreaming and vain thoughts which arise within us on account of our unbelief and imprudent worrying, and on account of vainglory, resentment, irritability and our other passions. With absolute faith let us rely entirely upon the Lord, and our many thoughts and empty dreams let us replace with unceasing prayer to the Lord Jesus. If we are still surrounded by enemies let us cry with strong weeping and mourning to the King of kings, just as people who have been wronged and persecuted cry out of a crowd. And if we are admitted to the King's inner apartment, let us present our complaint to Him and ask His mercy with the greatest quietness and humility, from the very depth of our soul. Such prayer is particularly powerful. It is entirely spiritual, expressed immediately to the very ear of the King, to His heart.

An indispensable, essential condition of success in the prayer of Jesus is the keeping of His commandments. *Remain in My love* (Jn. 15: 9), He said to His disciples. What does it mean to remain in love for the Lord? It means to remember Him unceasingly, to remain unceasingly in union with Him in spirit. The former without the latter is dead, and cannot even exist. *If you keep My commandments, you will remain in My love* (Jn. 15: 10). If we constantly observe the Lord's commandments, then by our spirit we shall be united with Him. If we are united with Him in spirit, we shall long for Him with our whole being, we shall unceasingly remember Him. Direct your actions, all your conduct by the commandments of the Lord Jesus, direct your words by them, direct your thoughts and feelings by them, and you will get to know the virtues of Jesus. When you feel within yourself these virtues by the action of divine grace, and when you acquire through these feelings an experimental knowledge of them, you will be ravished by the incorruptible sweetness which is not of this world or age, a gentle but powerful sweetness that annihilates the heart's inclination for all earthly enjoyments and pleasures. Having been ravished by the virtues of Jesus, you will love Him, and you will yearn for Him to dwell in you completely. Without Him you will regard yourself as perishing and lost. Then you will cry incessantly, cry from the fulness of conviction, with all your soul: *Lord Jesus Christ, Son of God, have mercy on me, a sinner.* The prayer of Jesus will replace all other prayers for you. And all of them—what thought can they contain and express more comprehensive than the thought of the pardon of sinners by Jesus?

Make your one aim in life the doing of the will of Jesus in every circumstance, however important or trifling it may seem. Try to do only what is pleasing to Jesus, and all your actions will be equally worthy of heaven. Love the will of Jesus more than the desires of your flesh, more than your ease and comforts, more than life, more than your soul. As often as possible read the Gospel, and learn in it the will of your Lord and Saviour. Do not disregard the smallest feature of the Gospel, not the least commandment however unimportant it may seem. Check and mortify all movements of your own, not only the sinful ones but also the apparently good ones which belong to fallen human nature, often very developed among pagans and heretics who are as far from the virtues of the Gospel *as the East is from the West* (Ps.

H

102: 12). Let all your old man be silent within you! Let Jesus alone act within you by His most holy commandments, and by the thoughts and feelings that arise from these commandments. If you live in this way, the prayer of Jesus will certainly blossom within you, quite independently of whether you dwell in the deepest solitude or amidst the noise of a community, because the place of abode and rest of this prayer is the mind and heart, renewed by the knowledge, experience and fulfilment of *the good and acceptable and perfect will of God* (Rom. 12: 2). Life according to the commandments of the Gospel is the one true source of spiritual progress, accessible to everyone who sincerely desires to succeed in whatever outward situation he may be placed by the inscrutable providence of God.

The practice of the prayer of Jesus by its very nature requires unbroken vigilance over oneself. "Reverent care," says St. Seraphim, "is needed here because *that sea*, that is, the heart with its thoughts and desires which must be purified by means of attention, *is great and stretches wide its arms; there are reptiles there without number* (Ps. 103: 25), that is, many vain, wrong and impure thoughts, the offspring of evil spirits."[1] We must keep constant watch over ourselves if we are to prevent sin from stealing in and ravaging our soul. But that is not enough. We must keep constant watch to see that our mind and heart remain in the will of Jesus and follow His holy orders, otherwise carnal wisdom may crowd out spiritual wisdom, or we may be carried away by some excitement or heating of the blood. We must try to remain as far as possible in a state of constant deadness, in a kind of fine coolness.[2] When this

---

[1] Instruction 5.
[2] Cp. 3 Kings 19 : 12.

feeling of a fine coolness makes its appearance, then the will of God is seen out of it more clearly and fulfilled more freely. When the will of God is seen more clearly, then hunger and thirst for divine righteousness is aroused with special force and with a profound realization of his poverty and with weeping the ascetic tries with renewed efforts to discover that righteousness within himself by the most attentive, most reverent prayer. "As this divine prayer," say Païssy Velitchkovsky, "is the highest of all monastic labours, the summit of reparations according to the decision of the Fathers, the source of virtues, a most subtle and invisible activity of the mind in the depth of the heart, therefore correspondingly invisible, subtle snares of various delusions and phantasies scarcely comprehensible for the human mind are set by the unseen enemy."[1]

It is impossible to lay another foundation for prayer by the name of Jesus other than the one laid, which is our Lord Jesus Christ Himself, the God-man. He incomprehensibly veiled the infinite Divine Nature with finite human nature, and from the finite human nature He displayed the actions of the infinite God. On account of our childishness the holy Fathers teach certain aids, as was said above, to make it easier for us to train ourselves to the prayer of Jesus. These aids are only aids and of no special import. We should not pay excessive attention to them, or attribute excessive importance to them. All the power, all the action and effect of the prayer of Jesus is due to the adorable and almighty name of Jesus, *the one name under heaven by which we must be saved* (Acts 4: 12). In order to become capable of discovering this action within us, we must be cultivated by the commandments of the Gospel, as the Lord

---

[1] Svitok, Ch. 4.

said: *Not everyone who says to Me, 'Lord, Lord,' shall
enter the kingdom of heaven,* either that which awaits us after
our death, or that which is discovered within us during our
earthly life, *but he who does the will of My Father Who is in
heaven* (Matt. 7: 21).

The proficient need no outward aids. Amidst the tur-
moil of a crowd they remain in silence. All the obstacles
to spiritual progress are within us—only in us! If anything
from without acts as an obstacle, it merely convicts and
exposes our feeble will, our duplicity, our corruption by sin.
No outward aids would be necessary if we lived as we ought
to live. Our life is slack, our will is fickle, our resolution is
negligible. And therefore we need outward aids, just as
those who have diseased legs need a stick and crutches.
The kind-hearted Fathers, seeing that I wish to practise the
prayer of Jesus, and seeing further that I am fully alive to
the world and that it acts powerfully upon me through my
senses, advise me to go into a solitary, dark cell for prayer,
so that in this way my senses may be rendered inactive, my
ties with the world may be severed, and my immersion
within myself may be facilitated. They advise me to sit
during the practice of the prayer of Jesus on a low stool so
that I may have the bodily position of a beggar asking for
alms, and may more easily feel the povery of my soul.
When I attend divine service and during the service engage
in the prayer of Jesus, the Fathers advise me to close my
eyes to guard me from distraction. That is becuase my
sight is alive to matter, and no sooner do I open my eyes
than I at once begin to receive in my mind the impressions
of objects that I see, which draw me away from prayer.
There are also many other outward aids which were discovered by men of prayer to provide material assistance in

mental activity. These aids can be used with profit, but in making use of them we must take into account the spiritual and bodily needs of each person. A mechanical aid which is very good for one ascetic may be useless and even harmful for another. The proficient refuse material aids just as a man healed of lameness throws away his crutch, just as a child on reaching a certain age refuses baby-clothes, just as from a finished house the scaffolding is taken away.

For all and everyone it is really useful *to begin* one's training in prayer by the name of the Lord Jesus by saying the prayer of Jesus *orally while enclosing the mind in the words of the prayer.* By the enclosure of the mind in the words of the prayer is meant the strictest attention to those words without which prayer is like a body without a soul. Let us leave it to our Lord Himself to transform our attentive oral prayer into mental prayer of the heart and soul. He will do this without fail when He sees us even a little purified, educated, matured, and prepared by the practice of the commandments of the Gospel. A prudent parent will not give a sharp sword to his infant son. A child is not in a position to use a sword against an enemy; he will play with a dangerous sword, and will lightly and easily pierce himself with it. A child in spiritual growth is unfit for spiritual gifts. He will use them not for the glory of God, not for the benefit of himself and his neighbours, not for defeating unseen foes; but he will use them to strike himself, will become conceited and filled with fatal pride and ruinous scorn for his neighbours. Even when we have no spiritual gifts, and are filled with stinking passions, we are proud of ourselves and boast, and do not cease to condemn and humiliate our neighbours who in all respects are better than we are! What would have happened if we had been entrusted with some spiritual wealth, some spiritual gift which singles out its possessor from his brethren and testifies that he is a chosen vessel of God? Would it not have become for us the cause of a terrible spiritual disaster?

Let us hasten to perfect ourselves in humility which consists in a specially blessed state of the heart and makes its appearance in the heart as a result of doing the commandments of the Gospel. Humility is that single altar on which it is allowed us by spiritual law to offer the sacrifice of prayer and on which the offered sacrifice of prayer ascends to God and appears before His face. Humility is that single vessel into which the gifts of grace are put by the finger of God.

Let us practise the prayer of Jesus disinterestedly, with simplicity and purity of intention, with penitence as our objective, with faith in God, with complete surrender to the will of God, with hope and trust in the wisdom, goodness and omnipotence of His holy will. In choosing the mechanical aids let us try to act with all possible care and prudence and not allow ourselves to be carried away by idle curiosity or irresponsible zeal which the inexperienced imagine to be a virtue but which the holy Fathers call proud audacity, mad impetuosity. Let us preferably resort to the simplest and humblest aids, since they are the safest. We repeat: all mechanical aids must be regarded merely as aids which have become useful for us on account of our weakness. Let us not put our hope either in them or in the quantity of our work lest we be robbed of our hope in the Lord and it prove that we put out trust essentially in ourselves or in something vain or material.

Let us not seek pleasure or visions. We are sinners unworthy of spiritual pleasures and visions, unfit for them on account of our decrepitude.[1] By attentive prayer let us seek to turn the gaze of our mind to ourselves so that we may discover within ourselves our sinfulness. When we discover it, let us stand mentally before our Lord Jesus Christ in the company of the lepers, the blind, the deaf, the lame, the paralysed, the possessed; and let us begin our mournful cry of prayer before Him from the poverty of our spirit and from a heart crushed with sorrow for our sinfulness. Let this cry be infinitely abundant. Let all prolixity and all variety of words prove unfit to express it. On account of its abundance and inexpressibility, let it be clothed continually; let it be clothed in the brief but meaningful prayer: *Lord Jesus Christ, Son of God, have mercy on me, a sinner.* Amen.

---

[1] "Decrepitude." Or: oldness, old self, old nature, old man (cp. Rom. 6: 6; Ephes. 4: 22; Col. 3: 9). That is to say, we need rejuvenation, regeneration.